D0598059

# NONPROFITS

 **made easy**

# Additional Titles in Entrepreneur's Made Easy Series

Entrepreneur
MAGAZINE'S

# NONPROFITS

## made easy

## Entrepreneur Press and David H. Bangs Jr.

EP Entrepreneur Press

Editorial Director: Jere Calmes
Cover Design: Beth Hansen-Winter
Editorial and Production Services: CWL Publishing Enterprises, Inc., Madison, Wisconsin, www.cwlpub.com

This publication is designed to provide accurate and authoritative information in regard to the subject matter covered. It is sold with the understanding that the publisher is not engaged in rendering legal, accounting, or other professional services. If legal advice or other expert assistance is required, the services of a competent professional person should be sought.

—From a Declaration of Principles jointly adopted by a Committee of the American Bar Association and a Committee of Publishers and Associations

ISBN 978-193253173-2
ISBN 1-932531-73-4

**Library of Congress Cataloging-in-Publication Data**
Bangs, David H.
  Nonprofits made easy / by Entrepreneur Press and David H. Bangs, Jr.
    p. cm.
  ISBN 1-932531-73-4 (alk. paper)
  1. Nonprofit organizations--Management.  I. Entrepreneur Press. II. Title.
  HD62.6.B36 2006
  658'.048—dc22
                                                              2006020658

Printed in Canada

11  10  09  08  07                                    10  9  8  7  6  5  4  3  2

HELP
HERE

# Contents

# Foreword

W HEN I FIRST MET DAVID (ANDY) BANGS IN 1999, I WAS THE
Executive Director of a lean, two-person arts organization. He was a consultant hired to help us develop our
first-ever business plan. The organization had a dedicated but small board of directors, and we were overwhelmed with requests for programs. It was clear we needed to recruit
additional board members and hire staff, but we were stuck in a six-month
planning cycle that endangered our growth.

Andy helped us define our understanding of constituencies and competition as well as help us develop cost analyses and cash flow projections in order
to develop a three-year business plan that included realistic operational goals.
Having a clearly articulated plan in place made it easier for us to recruit tal-
ented staff and new board members with appropriate skill sets. It was then
possible to keep everyone focused and moving forward.

As you will read in *Nonprofits Made Easy*, starting and sustaining a nonprofit requires a dedicated team invested in the organization. Successful nonprofits have the systems to support long-term planning and adequate
evaluation of progress against agreed-upon benchmarks. As you grow, this
allows staff, board, and volunteers working together to reach goals and celebrate the small victories along the way. The organizations that survive and
thrive are the ones that catch mistakes early, seek advice and solutions, and
change course swiftly.

We have been using Andy's books for years now and appreciate his ability to break down what could be a daunting task into manageable components, as he does in *Nonprofits Made Easy*. The nonprofit sector is fortunate to have this book available. A strong team of people armed with a clear vision and the appropriate tools can, in fact, make creating and sustaining a successful organization look easy. Good luck with your venture, have fun, and remember to celebrate the successes!

—Cynthia Billings
Executive Director of PlusTime NH
Chichester, NH

—Janice Hastings
Consultant to PlusTime NH
former Executive Director of VSA Arts
New Hampshire
former Director of Affiliate and Education
Services for VSA Arts, Washington, DC

HELP
HERE

# Introduction

I N 1999 THE NEW HAMPSHIRE CHARITABLE FOUNDATION (NHCF) SELECTED four nonprofit organizations to participate in the Entrepreneurial Investing (EI) program. Among the selection criteria were that the non-profits must:

► Have strong, well-established executive directors;

► Have potential for the organization to grow statewide;

► Have a history of achievement;

► Be small enough for a grant promising $30,000 to $35,000 a year for three years to make a big difference.

Two very small organizations (PlusTime NH and VSA Arts NH) were selected. As it turned out, they benefited more from the program than the two larger organizations (MicroCredit and Bancroft Industries), perhaps because they were smaller and newer. These four organizations were chosen from over 70 applicants and committed themselves to a close relationship with NHCF. As Pat Vasbinder, the COO of NHCF, put it, the foundation staff would become their new best friends.

Why was EI created? Major funders have been looking for precise outcomes from nonprofits. Goals of "making the community better" or "helping the poor feed themselves," while worthy, have to be expressed as objective outcomes so that progress can be measured. Business owners new to philanthropy have begun to ask for the same kind of accountability as they face in their businesses: financial goals, business plans, and measurable achievements. Hard numbers rather than soft goals are now mandatory. Many nonprofits are at a loss as to how to meet these new challenges.

EI had five aims. The first was to build capacity in these organizations (provide new skills, access to NHCF's wide range of experience, spot funding for needed consultants, and so forth). The second aim was to help develop a peer group of executive directors (EDs) so they could pool their skills. (This turned out to be one of the most valuable results of EI.) Third was to help the nonprofits to learn how to "talk business." If business owners are the funders of the future, the EDs have to be able to talk with the owners in terms the owners understand. Fourth, all small nonprofits have to widen their funding base, not just rely on the same few sources. In some cases this means that they have to develop a business that helps fund the organization. Finally, the fifth aim was to help the selected nonprofits make a change in the entire state, not just in a small local area.

To achieve these five aims, Pat and the NHCF staff decided to start EI with a six-month business planning program. I was hired to teach business planning to the four executive directors and whomever they chose to join them—board members, trusted staff, and in one case a friend.

The program was a revelation to all concerned. I gained a new and deeper appreciation of the difficulties the EDs face on a daily basis. Their ability to improvise and make do with limited resources impressed me. Their eagerness to pick up new skills (notably cash flow budgeting and strategic planning) delighted me. No teacher ever has had such eager students.

The people from PlusTime and VSA Arts were the most eager learners, perhaps because they had the most to learn. The idea that they could take control of their future rather than react to whatever grant opportunities presented themselves was a new one: the old habits made looking ahead almost impossible. Janice Hastings, then the head of VSA Arts NH, took to the rigors of financial management as fast as anyone I've met in 30 years of preaching cash flow and budgeting. Cynthia Billings, the ED of PlusTime, involved her board from the beginning and, as a result, was able to put her organization on a firm financial footing for the first time.

I'd be hard pressed to pick one over the other. The proof is in the progress their organizations made. Both of them quickly grew to statewide and both became models for similar organizations on a national level. Janice now spreads the planning gospel through VSA National, helping VSA affiliates in many states experience the joys of unit cost analysis. Cynthia has become a national power in the after-school movement. Could they have done this without EI? Of course. But they probably would not have done so well so quickly without it.

The hand-to-mouth management of small nonprofits is not a joke. It is common. I've seen nonprofits run on their ED's personal home equity line. I've seen others with no planning (business, operational, strategic, or financial) needlessly struggle simply to survive. (Pat and I referred to this as "climbing an ice cliff using well trimmed fingernails": an exercise in frustration.) Others have a constant struggle defining board and staff duties and relations. Yet others hurtle from one set of directives to the next, the ED spending 70 percent of her or his time looking for money rather than managing the organization. In one notable case there was no ED, no treasurer or financial manager, and a staff that frequently went unpaid but still bought supplies out of their own pockets.

Enough of that. The purpose of this book is to help people involved with small nonprofits make those organizations stronger by making better management decisions. Many small nonprofits are run by people who have a passion to make the world better in some way but who have little or no training in running a nonprofit organization. This book is for them, whether ED, staff, board member, or friend.

—David H. Bangs
Portsmouth NH

# Chapter 1

# Before Start-up

TO PROVIDE THE BEST LAUNCH FOR YOUR NONPROFIT ORGANIZATION, (NPO) start to keep track of your thoughts a year or so before start-up. Get a three-ring binder. You will use this to organize and keep track of all the information, ideas, and legalities that go into a successful start-up. You might use a computer (almost everyone does), but a three-ring binder is easier to flip through. Print out your thoughts and insights. They will change over time. As conditions shift, ideas that you once discarded for good reasons may come back into favor. The binder provides a historical record that will help you clarify your thoughts in the future. You will want to rethink some of the ideas you'll grapple with over the next several months, make changes, and keep track of the way these changes are made. Don't trust your memory. As Lao-Tse put it, the finest memory is not so firm as faded ink.

Ask yourself questions, write down your answers, and move on. The process is self-correcting—that is, you will change your answers as you go along. Starting an NPO is such an intriguing activity that this process is a lot of fun. Your ideas change, you change, and your organization will ultimately be the better for it.

Evaluating the ideas you come up with involves more than a feasibility analysis. You have to decide whether you want to be fully involved for

## Constructive Daydreaming

Use "constructive daydreaming" to set organizational goals that are consistent with your personal goals.

Daydreams play an interesting and important role in starting an NPO. First, the initial idea to start a nonprofit often comes in the form of a daydream: What if musical education were free to all students in this city? What would it be like to run that program? I know I could improve on this program. Here's what I'd do.

Second, constructive daydreaming is a terrific technique to try out the fit between organizational and personal goals. Form a sketch of your organization that you can fill in as you go along. Imagine going to the agency every day. What are you doing? How does it feel? What do you do when you aren't at the office? And so on. Your organization is going to be an extension of your own personality, no matter how hard you try to make it something else, so it makes good sense to look ahead. If the picture doesn't feel right, chances are excellent that there is a disparity between what you want to do and what the organization, as you project it, makes you do. You'll have plenty of compromises to make without setting the stage for long-term, self-defeating behavior. Running an NPO to achieve goals you are not passionate about is stupid. Projecting the future doesn't determine the future, but it does help you twist the odds in your favor.

years to come or would prefer a less involved role. Much of the evaluating process works by elimination. Does this idea fit? Does it meet my criteria? The more explicit you are about your selection criteria, the better your final choice will be.

Get a blank calendar. Careful management begins with setting time-bound goals. Goals always have a due date (by definition), hence the need for a calendar. You may want to use software to keep track of due dates and other goal-related points.

Here are a few questions to get you started:

**1. What is your nonprofit's mission?** This is the hardest question you will have to answer. Why? Your mission defines the scope of the enterprise, the kind of resources needed (people as well as money), where the nonprofit will be located, and how the mission might be accomplished. Since the mission is so central to the management of the nonprofit, it will receive lots of attention. For now, just jot down what you want the organization to achieve. You will refine the mission later.

**2. How large should the organization be?** The size of the organization depends on the mission. Some organizations are inherently limited in potential, while others have a chance for unlimited growth. A local charitable foundation is not likely to compete with the Gates or Rockefeller Foundations. The anticipated scale of your prospective NPO is an important factor in planning.

**3. What programs or services will you offer?** These must further the mission of the organization and, while they may generate money, chances are that they will need to be funded.

**4. Where will the services or programs be delivered?** Will you centralize services and programs or conduct them where the clients are?

**5. What will your role be?** The skills required to start an organization are different from those required to run it on a daily basis. Starting a nonprofit calls for entrepreneurial talents, not managerial skills. The two are rarely combined in one person.

*Starting a nonprofit calls for entrepreneurial talents, not managerial skills. The two are rarely combined in one person.*

**6. What are your qualifications for managing a nonprofit?** Experience in business is helpful, but not everyone can make a graceful transition from running a business to running a nonprofit. Experience in nonprofits is a plus. If you have been on a nonprofit board, you have an inkling of the ongoing problems that nonprofits face. If you don't have such experience, your work will be harder than necessary. Reading books and articles is a poor substitute for hands-on experience. Furthermore, donors (both individual and institutional) consider the experience of the board of directors and the executive director a major factor in making funding decisions.

**7. What level of commitment are you willing to make?** A part-time effort will, all things being equal, produce a part-time result. True, there are part-time nonprofits, such as Christmas gift drives, that are part-time by design. But most nonprofits call for a full-time commitment.

**8. What resources are you willing to commit to the nonprofit?** It takes longer to fund a nonprofit than to fund a business. You may find that you have to be the first backer. In fact it's likely, since potential donors will ask who else has put money into the organization.

# Check for Duplication of Efforts

Chances are slim that other people in other places haven't already addressed the problem you are trying to resolve. You can learn from them. Check to make sure that there is no organization already at work on the problem in your locale. For a wider search, use your Internet skills. You can

Google keywords describing your nonprofit. (For example, Google the three words "women," "business," and "education" and see what comes up.) A program that works in Alaska might be modified to succeed in Iowa. Duplication of efforts wastes time and resources, yet is all too common in the nonprofit sector.

Answer the following questions:

1. *Who else is addressing this problem?* Your local United Way is a good place to start answering this. That organization keeps track of local nonprofits. Visit every agency that might be dealing with the perceived problem. You'll meet some interesting people, pick up ideas and local information, and probably forge helpful alliances. The nonprofit network is powerful. Most executive directors interact with their peers regularly.
2. *If nobody is addressing the problem, why not?* The problem may be trivial or has already been solved. This is a precautionary step. You may want to go ahead anyway.
3. *Why is a new organization needed?* Could an existing organization address the problem? Make sure to ask the people you meet in the nonprofit world about this. There may be an organization that could become a fiscal sponsor for your nascent organization or, less formally, provide a home for the programs that you want to test.

## Fiscal Sponsor

A fiscal sponsor accepts and manages funds for the sponsored organization. Some of the usual requirements for the sponsored organization are:

- ▶ It must fit closely with the sponsor's mission.
- ▶ The board of directors of the sponsor must approve the arrangement.
- ▶ A legal contract or memo of understanding should lay out the duties and obligations of both parties.
- ▶ The sponsor may charge a determined percentage of the project's revenues.
- ▶ Contributions to the sponsor must be earmarked specifically to your organization.

# What Are the Risks?

Make a preliminary assessment of the risks. There are four major areas of risk: personal, business, market, and financial.

## Personal Risks

Personal risks are those that you run as an individual. If the organization will require a major commitment of your time, you might want to think about career risks. What if the venture fails? What will this do to your career prospects? (And if it succeeds, will it become your full-time career?) How does your family view the venture? A supportive family can make a difference; an unsupportive family can undermine your efforts. Do you face any financial risks in addition to interrupting your income from your current career? How much ego will you invest in the process? Finally, how might the success or failure of the organization affect your personal goals?

Here are some additional questions to consider:

▶ *What do I do well?* Most of us tend to be good at only a few of the tasks running an NPO requires. For example, you might be strong in generating new ideas but weak at finance, or terrific at managing people but hopeless at marketing. Knowing your strengths and weaknesses helps you balance and hence manage your organization. You will want to hire people with the specific skills you lack (or rent their skills as needed) in order to concentrate on doing what you do best.

▶ *What do I like to do?* About the best tip-off to what you do best is to look at what you like to do. What have you enjoyed doing in the past? Do you like to initiate actions, or do you prefer to follow a clear set of directions? Do you prefer to do things yourself, or do you like to delegate and control? You may be able to organize your new NPO to allow you to do what you like to do most—and minimize the time spent doing things you loathe. You will work harder, longer, and with more enjoyment at work that interests you. Work that you don't like you will, over time, do grudgingly and less thoroughly. The ultimate cost to your NPO will be higher than it would be if you knew in the first place what you don't like to do and then paid someone else to do those tasks. That doesn't mean that you won't have to do a lot of things that aren't fun. Wait until you have to fire an employee—a task you can't delegate.

▶ *What would I like to be doing five years from now?* A five-year horizon is a useful defining tool. In five years you might wish to start another NPO, or manage a much larger one, or devote your time to research. Whatever. Use the five-year test to help understand what you like to do. If you're working toward a goal (not necessarily financial, though financial goals are important, too), the day-to-day frustrations

*You will want to hire people with the specific skills you lack (or rent their skills as needed) in order to concentrate on doing what you do best.*

5

of management are easier to handle. The five-year horizon also helps you define some benchmarks and a plan for attaining them. Maybe you want to be able to spend more time with your family, do community work, or get involved in some other activity.

▶ *How will I get out of the organization?* It's never too early to begin thinking about an exit strategy. Sooner or later you'll come to a point at which you have to leave the NPO. A succession plan will become important when you start soliciting major grants.

## Business Risks

Is there really an opportunity? Will you be serving a real need and at the same time be able to maintain the organization's vitality? Can you put together a staff and gather the needed resources? These questions are about the viability of the organization.

*Since your NPO will almost surely become reliant on donations and grants, start thinking now about what emotional hooks your NPO might use.*

Note that some causes are easier to fund than others. Causes that the public is passionate about, such as protecting animals or children, lend themselves to strong emotional appeals. Causes that are less emotionally wrenching look for a "poster child" to add emotional appeal to their fundraising and awareness programs. Since your NPO will almost surely become reliant on donations and grants, start thinking now about what emotional hooks your NPO might use.

## Market Risks

At the very least you want to be sure that there will be enough clients (those who receive your services) to warrant the effort that you will be making. What are the trends — is the problem getting worse? Are more people paying attention to it? How will you tailor your services (and products, if any) to the needs and desires of both clients and donors?

## Financial Risks

You have to know what your start-up costs will be. What will basic legal and licensing costs be for deposits and rents, salaries and benefits, and all the costs of running an organization?

Where will you get the necessary funds? Your assets? Funding sources such as foundations and charities and grants? Individual donors? Will these sources be available long term? Successful start-ups depend on a balance of resources and managerial experience. Ask yourself these questions and jot down your answers:

▶ *How much money can I invest?* All organizations run on cash during the start-up period. Many NPOs are started with a combination of savings and "house money." The amount required will vary from one NPO to the next and will depend to some degree on your depth of experience. The less experience the more capital is required to provide a margin for the inevitable errors made during start-up.

▶ *Can I and should I attract other donors?* Even if you have enough cash without involving other donors, don't go it alone. You want to have other donors (including those who loan you money at this stage) to establish credibility with the community, help by becoming board members, and put together a strong management team.

Make sure you consider how your new venture will affect the following:

▶ Your *income*. Unless you are able to retain your full-time job and start your NPO as a part-time enterprise, your income will suffer. Start-up organizations seldom provide any salary to the founder right away. Save some money to plug this gap. A second income (a supportive spouse, in many cases) can also make a big difference.

▶ Your *hours*. Starting any organization devours time. In the first few months of an NPO, when everything is new and shortcuts haven't been discovered, you'll live your organization. You'll think about it all the time, whether at the office or not. Your time will not be your own— one of the biggest problems newcomers to managing small NPOs face is that they can't close the door at 5 o'clock and go home. They lug the NPO and its problems with them. So will you.

▶ Your *support level*. Wholehearted support from family and friends helps you avoid burnout. Your family and friends have a sizeable emotional investment in you and your organization. Let them help and they will. They will understand the demands on you better, which in turn will allay their concerns about the amount of time, effort, and worry you put into your start-up. People who take an intelligent interest in your organization can provide you with objective advice and criticism. To get this kind of support, keep them informed from the start. Don't keep everything to yourself. If you are worried, tell them. If you are uncertain, tell them.

*Your family and friends have a sizeable emotional investment in you and your organization. Let them help and they will.*

▶ Your *commitment to family, community, personal activities*. Many social entrepreneurs find that the lack of time for family, community, and personal activities (hobbies, sports, reading, and so on) is the high-

7

est price they pay for leadership. During the start-up period, this price is reasonable. Later, when the NPO is actually going, lack of time becomes a leading cause of burnout. At this point, make sure you have a clear picture of what your commitments will be, how long they'll take to fulfill, and what sacrifices (if any) you'll have to make.

Some other factors you should consider:

▶ Some organizations are more limiting than others. A homeless shelter requires someone with authority (perhaps you) on-site 24/7. The hours are long, the rewards high—but it may not be a good choice if you place a premium on family or community activities.

▶ A shaky marriage or other relationship is never improved by starting an organization. Don't expect to lose yourself in your start-up and magically come out of it with a better relationship.

▶ Starting your NPO should be a positive and exciting experience. Negative motivations don't last. Positive motivations do. That's why it is so important to place your personal goals ahead of your business goals. Your NPO should at least parallel your goals.

You need answers to all of these questions. Then be aware of them and come up with estimates that you can test and specify more exactly. Use this checklist to help you.

| Personal |
| --- |
| Business |
| Market |
| Financial |

**Figure 1-1.** Checklist of risks

## Nonprofits

What is a nonprofit organization? And what are the benefits?

The most common nonprofit is a 501(c)(3), defined as "a religious, educational, charitable, scientific, literary, testing for public safety, fostering national or international sports competition or preventing cruelty to children or animals." While there are other forms of nonprofits (see Figure 1-2), this book is concerned with 501(c)(3)s only.

The main benefits of becoming a 501(c)(3) include:

▶ Exemption from federal income tax
▶ Exemption from the Federal Unemployment Tax Act (FUTA)
▶ Ability to accept contributions that are tax-deductible to the donor
▶ Eligibility for government and foundation grants
▶ Eligibility for bulk mailing permits
▶ Possibly eligibility for some local and state tax exemptions

Since there are variations from one state and locality to the next, it is prudent to get legal and accounting advice.

| 501(c)(3) | 501(c)(4) | 501(c)(6) | 501(c)(7) |
|---|---|---|---|
| Organizational requirement | No requirement (or less stringent) | No requirement (or less stringent) | No requirement (or less stringent) |
| Assets must be dedicated to charitable purposes | No requirement to dedicate assets | No requirement to dedicate assets | No requirement to dedicate assets |
| Social activities must be insubstantial | Social activity may be anything less than "primary" | Social activity may be anything less than "primary" | Social activity must be primary; other activities must be less than primary |
| Legislative activity must be insubstantial or less than 20% if election made | No limit on legislative activity as long as it furthers the exempt purpose | No limit on legislative activity as long as it furthers the exempt purpose; legislative expenditures may limit the deductibility of dues | No limit on legislative activity as long as it furthers the exempt purpose |
| Absolute prohibition against political activity | Political activity permitted, but taxed | Political activity permitted, but taxed | Political activity permitted, but taxed |

**Figure 1-2.** Comparison of 501(c)(3) and other nonprofits (continued on next page)

| 501(c)(3) | 501(c)(4) | 501(c)(6) | 501(c)(7) |
|---|---|---|---|
| Must serve public purposes | Can serve community purposes, can be somewhat narrower than (c)(3) | Can serve the business purposes of the members | Serves the social and recreation purposes of members |
| Donations are deductible as charitable contributions by donors on their tax returns | Donations not deductible as charitable contributions; businesses sometimes deduct as advertising | Donations not deductible as charitable contributions; businesses sometimes deduct as advertising; dues may be deductible as business expense | Donations not deductible as charitable contributions |
| Eligible for low cost nonprofit bulk mailing permit | Not eligible for lowest bulk mail rates | Not eligible for lowest bulk mail rates | Not eligible for lowest bulk mail rates |
| Must take care to generate enough public support to avoid classification as a private foundation | Not an issue under (c)(4) | Not an issue under (c)(6) | Not an issue under (c)(7) |
| Exempt from federal income tax unless the organization has unrelated business income | Exempt from federal income tax unless the organization has unrelated business income | Exempt from federal income tax unless the organization has unrelated business income | Exempt from federal income tax on income derived from members; other income taxed |

**Figure 1-2.** Comparison of 501(c)(3) and other nonprofits (continued)

# Refine Your Ideas

*The passion you bring to the NPO will be a major factor in its long-term success.*

You already have a pretty clear idea of what your NPO will be. Use the next six months to clarify this picture, make it sharper and better focused, test your assumptions, and improve your business management skills.

Note that at this point you can influence the nature of the NPO. Once you have invested substantial cash and effort, your choices will be much more limited. Make sure that the organization you want to start is indeed right for you. Starting an organization that reflects your interests and personal goals makes more sense than starting one that is only mildly interesting to you. The passion you bring to the NPO will be a major factor in its long-term success.

Look at all kinds of nonprofits that are doing work similar to what you propose to do. For example, if you are interested in opening an agency that works with children after school, check out as many different after-school programs as you can. All will have something of value for you. The wider the range of your search, the better your final choice will be and the more information you will acquire. You will also meet a lot of people who will help you define the mission of your NPO and know who else deals with the kinds of problems you wish to address.

# Begin Your Research

Information sources come in two varieties: "hot" and "cool." You need both kinds.

"Hot" information sources are interpersonal and interactive and provide immediate feedback. Activities such as talking with people, including those whom you may be soliciting for funds or trying to persuade to join your Board of Directors, taking classes in nonprofit management, and interviewing prospective clients all yield hot information.

Balance this with "cool" information. Cool sources are less interactive, more academic. Reading books and journals, running down ideas on the Internet, even attending lectures are good examples of cool information sources. Although these activities are not interactive, they provide high information value for the time invested.

## Get Hot Information

If possible, get experience working in nonprofit management. While this is not always an option, you can't beat it for value. You learn the tricks of the trade, the jargon, and when and where problems tend to crop up. You get to know funders, donors, suppliers, and clients—and how to keep the clients happy. And you get paid while doing so.

If you can, serve on the board of one or more nonprofits. The problems are generic: the never-ending search for money, the difficult task of getting into the public consciousness ("social marketing"), the extraordinary nonprofit competition for employees. Ideally, put in time as the board treasurer. Financial expertise is vitally important in the nonprofit world.

Talk with nonprofit board members, executives, and managers. Ask a lot of questions: What's different about your organization? What's good or bad about it? What's the future? What kinds of problems do you encounter?

*Ideally, put in time as the board treasurer. Financial expertise is vitally important in the nonprofit world.*

11

What barriers to raising money have you encountered?

Seek out experts and other helpful hot information sources. Structure a list of questions, to make sure that you don't impose on their time and you get the most valuable information. Take notes. Hot information melts away if you don't write it down.

Here are some other great hot information sources:

▶ *Nonprofits similar to yours in locations that don't compete with you.* Take a trip and seek out nonprofit managers. Tell them what you're doing and point out that you won't be competing with them. The magic phrase, "I've got a problem and I think you can help me," opens many doors. You will always get a better reception if you make an appointment, tell them how long it will take, and submit a list of questions (see below) that you will ask. In fact, this is a good technique for anyone whom you would like to interview, since it puts some boundaries on the visit and gives them a chance to prepare.

▶ *Competitors.* Your competitors will be willing to talk with you. Try them. The worst they can do is lie to you! It may seem odd to think of nonprofit organizations as competitors. It isn't. You will compete for money, personnel, supporters, and top-of-mind awareness. The nonprofit world is very cooperative and supportive, fortunately, and you have a special appeal if you make it clear from the start that you want to be a collaborator, not a threat. But you will still be competing with them.

▶ *Trade shows.* Attend them—they are a great information source. Many of the suppliers and consultants to the nonprofit world will be there as well as many nonprofits. It's one-stop shopping for hot information sources.

▶ *Trade association executives and editors, consultants to the industry, executives of charitable foundations and philanthropies, and career counselors in the industry.* Anyone with direct connections to the nonprofit world will have useful insights. Make sure to get in touch with these people.

▶ *SCORE* (Service Corps of Retired Executives). This national organization provides management seminars and direct consulting services to nonprofits in all stages of growth.

▶ *SBDCs* (Small Business Development Centers). If there's an SBDC in your area, make full use of it. Their expertise and willingness to help are especially useful when it comes time to write your business plan. They provide direct consulting services and are a most effective link to other sources of information and assistance.

*The nonprofit world is very cooperative and supportive, fortunately, and you have a special appeal if you make it clear from the start that you want to be a collaborator, not a threat.*

## Sample Questions

These are questions I tend to ask. You don't have to follow every bit of advice; in fact, you cannot, since it will often be inconsistent. Your goal is to become aware of tricks of the trade you should know.

1. What were your biggest start-up problems? What special problems did you have after a year of operations?
2. If you knew then what you know now, what would you have done differently?
3. How long does it take to get bank credit? What do bankers look for when analyzing a nonprofit? Who are the most helpful local bankers?
4. What are the best information sources for a NPO like this?
5. What kind of funding problems should I expect during my start-up year?
6. What kind of computers and software programs do you use? Why? What would you recommend that I use? (Be specific. Ask about financial, fundraising, database, and other management software.)
7. What community organizations (Rotary, Kiwanis, etc.) do you find most valuable?
8. What kind of training should I get? What should I provide?
9. Are there any special start-up problems I should look out for?
10. What do you like best about running a nonprofit? What do you dislike most?

▶ *Local business schools.* Many professors are involved with small nonprofits. As a side benefit, professors are often willing to sit on the board of a small nonprofit. Most colleges and universities offer courses in nonprofit management that may be helpful to you and your board members.

▶ *Your local Chamber of Commerce.* It acts as a clearinghouse for many programs and will give you directions whether you are a member or not. Since you will be seeking community awareness of your NPO, it behooves you to become active in the Chamber. Your involvement will pay high dividends.

# Get Cool Information

Books, lectures, and other activities with low or no interactivity tend to be more solitary and analytic than hot information sources, but don't ignore their value. In the trade, these are called "secondary sources."

Start with your local librarian. He or she will help organize and plan your research. If there's a business library or a business school library nearby, visit and ask for help.

The Internet has become the number-one source of cool information. The main problem with the net is the sheer amount of information available. (Googling "nonprofit associations" brings up 15,800,000 references. Googling "social marketing" yields 107,000,000 hits! If you are new to the nonprofit world, you'd best stick to a very few Internet sources, such as BoardSource (*www.boardsource.org*) or the very highly regarded Georgia Center for Nonprofits (*www.gcn.org*). Otherwise you'll just spin your wheels.

Trade publications and trade association publications, especially periodicals (print, electronic, or online), can be very informative. Here are some to consider:

*The Chronicle of Philanthropy*
www.philanthropy.com

*The NonProfit Times*
www.nptimes.com

*Nonprofit Issues*
www.nonprofitissues.com

*Non-Profit Nuts & Bolts*
www.nutsbolts.com

*Nonprofit World*
Society for Nonprofit Organizations
www.snpo.org

*Contributions Magazine*
www.contributionsmagazine.com

Set up clip files to organize the information you gather. Manila folders and some paper and pencils are all you need. Take notes on those articles or books you can't clip. The database you build over a period of a few weeks saves you months of work later on. A lot of basic demographic and market research can be gleaned from magazines and journals. Once more, ask your librarian for help.

# Build Your Skills by Taking Formal Management Courses

Formal management courses are a fast way up the learning curve if you've had little management experience. Remember: there is no prize given for reinventing standard management practices that have evolved over years of painstaking effort by millions of intelligent people.

- ▶ *Check out your state's nonprofit center.* New Hampshire's Center for Nonprofits (*www.nhnonprofits.org*) provides courses, counseling, workshops, and other events. The odds are that your state has a similar organization. Check the Resources in Chapter 10.

- ▶ *Attend a SCORE pre-business workshop.* This one's a must. A pre-business workshop helps you even before you start your business plan. Its greatest value lies in the interaction with other people facing similar start-up fears and concerns. Call SCORE and ask when their next pre-business seminar takes place. The cost is trivial. The payoff is immense.

- ▶ *Check with the nearest Small Business Development Center (SBDC).* SBDCs run seminars for small businesses and participate in business association programs run by other groups. (Check the "SBDC Locator" on the Web site at *www.sba.gov/sbdc.*) Their help is direct, hands-on, and usually one-on-one. Nonprofits are welcome; the business core is very closely related to the core of for-profits in almost all respects.

- ▶ *Find out about SBA-sponsored seminars and short courses.* The SBA sponsors numerous short, intensive, problem-specific courses including one for people planning to start or manage nonprofits. (Check "News & Events" by state on the Web site at *www.sba.gov.*)

- ▶ *Check with local colleges for extension programs.* Include vocational and technical schools; they often provide down-to-earth seminars and workshops—more practical, less academic.

- ▶ *Look into programs sponsored by trade associations*, often found at trade shows or in conjunction with regional business expositions. You don't have to be a member of the trade association to attend these. Just get on the mailing list by subscribing to the trade magazines in areas relevant to your organization.

- ▶ B*ecome familiar with "high-tech" solutions to problems in your line of*

*Formal management courses are a fast way up the learning curve if you've had little management experience.*

*business*. No intelligent NPO executive director should try to run his or her organization without taking full advantage of up-to-date software. If you are not computer literate, become computer literate and comfortable as soon as possible. There are excellent software packages for fundraising (Blackbaud, Inc., *www.blackbaud.com*, for example). Accounting and other financial tools are readily available. And you can't manage a large and growing database economically without the right software.

*Use the year before starting your NPO to visualize it, in detail, including its impact on your personal life.*

Use the year before starting your NPO to visualize it, in detail, including its impact on your personal life. Take skill-building courses and conduct basic research to improve your odds. This includes both interactive and solitary research. Become aware of and use the many federal and state programs that have been established to help people start businesses. And don't fail to take your local librarian out to lunch: he or she has highly professional skills and knows how to do research. Business owners seldom call upon librarians, but your local librarian can be extraordinarily helpful to you in this research phase of your start-up.

## Expert Advice: Assess the Impact on Your Family and Personal Life

Starting an organization affects every facet of your life. There are always loose ends to tie up, work to do, and bills to pay. The result is that your family and social life will suffer. While this is usually a problem only until the organization settles into a routine, it is grave enough to make many enterprises fail. A supportive family and understanding friends go a long way toward making your organization a success.

The emotional ups and downs inherent in a start-up are unexpected and often severe. You'll find that periods of elation and excitement are followed by panic when grants receivable are slow to turn into cash, or a major benefactor dies unexpectedly, or your biggest donor decides to give elsewhere. If you are not used to the fluctuating fortunes of small nonprofit life, be aware. This is a problem that you will have to learn to live with.

# Starting a Nonprofit: Running Example

I will use the start-up and development of the Women's Business Center of New Hampshire (WBC) as a running example. I was involved with this organization from its roots in the Papoutsy Seminar for Women Entrepreneurs through the decision to make it a stand-alone 501(c)(3) in

1995. I remained on the board until the spring of 2003, by which time the WBC was running smoothly.

Chris Papoutsy, a New Hampshire entrepreneur and philanthropist, established The Papoutsy Seminar in 1993 to provide practical business advice to women in the Portsmouth, New Hampshire area. Quite simply, he spotted a problem and decided to do something about it. He put together a board of advisors, including educators, business owners, and the Greater Piscataqua Community Foundation (GPCF) in Portsmouth. Chris and his board of advisors decided that women faced barriers to business ownership that men did not. Two of the most obvious barriers were that women aren't socialized or educated to seek out business ownership and there was no equivalent of "the old boys' network" to provide support and advice.

Realistically, the Papoutsy Seminar could not change the barriers that women faced, but they could help a limited number of women get the tools to compete in business.

Chris and the board decided to co-sponsor a series of workshops with New Hampshire College (now Southern New Hampshire University) using its faculty and space. The initial program was competitive: women were asked to submit an application outlining their business idea to a panel that would select the most promising ideas.

The program was free. NHC and the GPCF treated it as any other program. Chris donated money to the GPCF (thus getting a tax deduction) and the GPCF funneled the funds to NHC. Chris picked up the tab for the teacher, supplies, and even coffee and Danish.

The results were encouraging. Fifteen women were selected from over 50 applicants. The program ran from December through May. Not one woman dropped out. Not all of the women went on to start their own businesses. The process of writing a business plan persuaded half of them to decide to either postpone or abandon their proposed business. That was OK: one of Chris's aims was to help the clients make sound business decisions. Several others changed their plans dramatically, another desirable result. Three started businesses. These were small enterprises, to be sure, but it was a start.

While the Papoutsy Seminar was not a 501(c)(3), Chris and his board carefully addressed the same questions as it makes sense to address for any new nonprofit program.

1. **What is your nonprofit's mission?** The mission of the Papoutsy Seminar was to educate Seacoast New Hampshire women about business ownership. This mission was a preliminary version that would change over time.

2. **How large should the organization be?** Very small. The only employee was Kate Kirkwood, an NHC professor whose involvement with the seminar was part-time.

3. **What programs or services will you offer?** Education to provide women with the business skills necessary to start or expand a business. The problems Chris and his board saw were being treated offhandedly, not directly.

4. **Where will the services or programs be delivered?** The alliance with NHC ensured that the seminars would be centralized.

5. **What will your role be?** Chris wisely chose to stay in the background. Using an advisory board is smart; it corrals a range of experience and ideas that no single person can have.

6. **What are your qualifications for managing a nonprofit?** Chris realized that running a nonprofit was hardly his ideal job. Part of his entrepreneurial success depended on being able to use experts and delegate authority, traits he carried over to the Papoutsy Seminar.

7. **What level of commitment are you willing to make?** The Papoutsy Seminar was set up as a part-time endeavor, meeting roughly every other week. If you can find an ally the way Chris did, it provides an excellent and low-cost way to test a concept. If the program had stayed small, it would probably still be hosted by Southern New Hampshire University.

8. **What resources are you willing to commit to the nonprofit?** Chris contributed money (always helpful), time, and energy to getting the programs up and running.

Chris ran little personal risk: he had an idea that he was willing to put to the test. If his idea worked, fine. If not, too bad; at least he'd have given it a try. The business risk was nil; there were women eager to avail themselves of the seminars and many proven models to emulate. A rising presence of women in small business ownership had been observed and quantified by the Small Business Administration. The costs were low (less than $5,000 for the first year, not counting the kick-off party) and Chris could well afford to make the initial donation and, if necessary, fund the program until it could stand on its own. The alliance with NHC and the GPCF was an intermediate step, a sponsorship, to use existing organizations rather than starting a brand new nonprofit. This was a test program that, once proven, led to the establishment of the WBC in 1995.

# Chapter 2

# Starting a Nonprofit

ENTREPRENEURS HAVE A MOTTO: READY! FIRE! AIM! AT SOME POINT IT is better to start something than to sit around and think about how it might be done. That's "Ready!" and "Fire!" "Aim!" comes soon thereafter. If you have the chance to get the kind of experience that we had with the Papoutsy Seminar, go for it. You'll learn more from doing than from any amount of reading and planning.

## Refine Your Mission Statement

Do you remember the children's game telephone, in which players line up, the leader whispers a statement to the first player, and each player in turn whispers it to the next, with the result being a statement that bears little resemblance to the original? The same thing happens when an organization doesn't have a clear mission statement.

Here are some tips for creating a useful mission statement. Get input from all your stakeholders. Try brainstorming, asking questions, and soliciting opinions about what is central to the organization's goals. For drafting the statement, use one writer, not a committee. Draft a statement and then run it by your stakeholders for comments. You are aiming for the 15-second elevator pitch—a short, succinct statement that will help you stay focused

## Mission Statement: Essential

Frances Hesselbein, former head of the Girl Scouts of America, told *Business Week* why mission statements are needed and how to formulate them:

> We kept asking ourselves very simple questions: What is our business? Who is our customer? And what does the customer consider value? We are really here for one reason: "to help a girl reach her highest potential." … More than any one thing, that made the difference. Because when you are clear about your mission, corporate goals and operating objectives flow from it. ("Profiting from the Nonprofits," *Business Week*, March 26, 1990)

Don't let the age of this quote put you off. These words are as true and clear now as they were then.

and avoid activities that aren't central to your mission. This is tricky. Your mission statement should be narrow enough to focus your efforts, broad enough to permit growth, and simple enough to remember. Otherwise it won't be used and won't be useful.

The key start-up question is "What business are you in?" Your answer will influence your plans. This in turn will determine what kinds of research will pay off best for you, what groups to join or ally yourself with, and even where to locate your NPO.

The immediate impulse is to answer, "I'm in the music education business" or "I provide health services to local uninsured people." These answers, built on products or markets, are beginnings of a mission statement.

*The aim is to define what business you are in, what you provide and to whom, and what makes your organization different—all in 25 words or less.*

The aim is to define what business you are in, what you provide and to whom, and what makes your organization different—all in 25 words or less. You will use the resulting mission statement to keep your focus on your primary business.

One of the biggest pitfalls for a new organization is to be unclear about its mission. As a result, efforts are scattered and fragmentary, many expensive and distracting false starts are made, and all too often the fledgling NPO is crippled.

Ask these questions:

1. What is our purpose?
2. What business are we in?
3. What problems do we want to address?
4. What services will we provide?
5. Who has these problems? (Who is our customer?)

## Stakeholders

Stakeholders are those people who have a strong interest in the organization. These include:

- ▶ Clients (customers)
- ▶ Board members
- ▶ Employees
- ▶ Volunteers
- ▶ Funders
- ▶ Suppliers
- ▶ Community members, especially local politicians
- ▶ Allies
- ▶ Supporters

You may have others to add to this list. Most nonprofits have more stakeholders than they realize. For example, whatever your services, "community members" stand to benefit from your efforts, even if indirectly.

6. Where are they?
7. What do they want—not what do you want to provide but rather what do they want you to provide?

Once you have short answers to these seven questions, pay special attention to the active verbs. These will form the guts of your mission statement.

## Vision Statement

Many nonprofits find a vision statement useful. In a vision statement, you paint a qualitative picture of what the world would be like if you were to achieve your mission. This can help frame the mission statement.

PlusTime NH's vision statement:

"PlusTime NH strives for a day when every community supports all its youth and families by providing access to quality after-school programs designed to promote the positive well-being of the whole child."

# Do Market Research

For-profit businesses use market research to try to identify and understand their customers (prospective and actual), and to understand the fit between those persons and the products and services offered, the differences among competing products and services, and how their customers want those goods

21

packaged and presented. Armed with this information, the astute owner can tailor the package of product, service, price, and presentation to the market, thus improving his or her chances of securing an adequate (profitable) share of the market.

For nonprofits, research is more complicated. You want to do all the above—but you also want to start making a comprehensive list of people who might become stakeholders—as employees, colleagues, board members, or significant supporters in the community. And while you want to become familiar with competitors (either direct or indirect), you also want to figure out which organizations might become your allies.

Do your market research systematically. Write down the information as you gain it. This gives you a base to build on and will help you when it comes time to write a business plan (see Chapter 8) and when you apply for grants and seek donations.

What questions do you need to answer?

**1. Who are your clients?** As a first step, ascertain who your clients (customers) are or will be. You must know and understand the people who will benefit from your services. Who are they? How many are there? Where are they? What services can you provide that they need and/or want? This is essential information. You will have to provide clear answers to satisfy the requirements of your funders (assuming that you will need outside funds).

**2. Select the right location.** Your mission drives the location. While it may be more convenient to locate your office at home, the real question is "Where do your clients need you to be?"

Another way to address the location issue is to determine how you will deliver your services. Will clients come to you? Will you go to them? Can your office be in one place while programs are delivered in another? Location may seem to be a simple matter, but it will affect staff, sources of funding (some philanthropies are restricted to tight local areas), and the level of service you provide.

Keep in mind that your Web site is a location too.

**3. Who are your competitors?** You will be competing for your share of public awareness (*top-of-mind* or *mindshare*). You will compete even more vigorously for funding: the more your competitors are similar to you, the more intense the competition, so your best allies will be often be aiming for the same grants.

Expect competition for employees as well, especially key employees. The pool of people interested in working for nonprofits is limited. Salaries are

*As a first step, ascertain who your clients (customers) are or will be. You must know and understand the people who will benefit from your services.*

## Colleague or Competitor?

"I don't have competitors, just colleagues." That's a common reaction among people in nonprofits. True, collaboration and cooperation among nonprofits is common and valuable. But your colleague agencies can be your fiercest competitors. This is not to say they are enemies, but consider the facts of the situation.

Charitable foundations, including United Way and other fund providers, have a limited amount of money at their disposal. Their job is to make the best use of their funds, which they do by carefully scrutinizing grant applications and other requests. Your closest allies will apply for those grants that fit their mission (sometimes a stretch). You probably will apply for many of the same grants.

On a local level, nonprofits are incestuous. People may serve on more than one board, volunteers sometimes or often work for two or more organizations, employees switch from one position to another. While this is healthy, it also presents challenges.

In the for-profit world, companies closely study their competitors. Nonprofits should follow that lead. This is an integral part of your market research. We suggest that you identify your five closest competitors.

always lower than in the private sector. People who share your passion for the nonprofit sector may be willing to accept the lower pay and tighter career path, but your fellow nonprofits have been and are seeking to identify these passionate people. Not surprisingly, once you are up and running, your staff may be raided by other agencies. You train and develop key staff … and then off they go. Turnover in nonprofits is a problem tied directly to competition.

As for volunteers, most nonprofits rely on volunteers for a wide range of duties. Your board of directors (see immediately below) will be composed of volunteers. Programs and fundraising events rely on volunteers: think of the people who help run road races or keep the local Little League going. Competition for these volunteers is intense and ongoing.

*Most nonprofits rely on volunteers for a wide range of duties. Competition for these volunteers is intense and ongoing.*

# Put Together a Board of Directors

**What does the board of directors do?** The board oversees all legal and financial activities of the organization, from incorporation and fundraising through hiring an executive director and setting personnel policies. It sets policies and makes sure that those policies are followed. It sets goals and makes plans to achieve those goals. Early in the nonprofit's life, the directors

## Three Duties of Board Members

Three kinds of board duties are often cited: the duty of *care* (which implies prudence), the duty of *loyalty* (to put the organization's welfare ahead of other considerations), and the duty of *obedience* (to act in accordance with the organization's mission, goals, and bylaws).

will be very hands-on, performing many of the duties that in a more mature organization would be done by staff: answering the phone, providing services, keeping the books, public relations, and so forth. As the organization matures, the directors will be less hands-on and exercise more oversight.

**How will you find board members?** Ask those persons you think could help you. They'll be flattered. The worst thing that could happen is that they'll say no. Talk with any of the following:

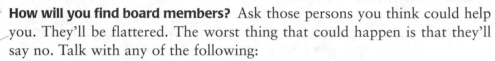

- ▶ Other nonprofits
- ▶ Business friends
- ▶ Former employers or supervisors
- ▶ Retired businesspeople from your industry
- ▶ Professionals
- ▶ Business professors
- ▶ Investors
- ▶ Consultants
- ▶ Experts in your field

You will benefit from their experience and contacts. Even a personal friend who can intelligently listen to you makes a good sounding board. Success comes from common sense and diligence. Outside advisors help you preserve both.

## Composition of the Board

Before recruiting board members, think long and hard about what the composition of the board should be. Most initial boards are composed of early supporters. That's fine; you need their energies and enthusiasm to get the nonprofit up and running. But there's a danger in that approach, as the board then has just one voice. A better way is to think about the skills you want on the board. See Figure 2-1 for ideas on how to do this.

As column heads, jot down the skills or other attributes that you seek in board candidates. The four suggested (nonprofit experience, financial, legal,

| | Nonprofit Board Experience | Financial | Legal | Community Leader | Other |
|---|---|---|---|---|---|
| Jere | | ✔ | | | |
| Andi | ✔ | | | ✔ | |
| Karen | ✔ | | | ✔ | |
| Charles | ✔ | | ✔ | | |
| | | | | | |

**Figure 2-1.** Board matrix

leadership) are just that: suggestions. Try to limit the skills to only the most important for your organization at this time.

Down the left, write down the names of people who you think might be or could become interested in joining the board. Since you have been diligently making a list of possible allies, you have a place to start.

Mark which of the indicated skills or other attributes each potential candidate would bring to the board. Now check for any major gaps in the skills and/or attributes your organization needs.

Aim for a balance of voices. For example, a CPA or banker will provide the cautious financial restraint that is needed for survival. Some boards have one or more lawyers, not so much for the legal advice they may provide (though that's helpful), but for their characteristic skepticism. You might wish for people with public relations and advertising skills, community leaders, client representatives, or people with fundraising and grant-writing expertise, or other skills. Other considerations include where the board members are recruited, age, sex, or other demographic criteria.

*Some boards have one or more lawyers, not so much for the legal advice they may provide (though that's helpful), but for their characteristic skepticism.*

## WBC: Board of Directors

The WBC started with its advisory board. The nucleus of the board of directors came from this group and included (deliberately) representatives from the Greater Piscataqua Community Foundation and New Hampshire College, a banker, two lawyers, and a CPA as well as a few friends of the Papoutsy Seminar. All had some experience serving on nonprofit boards and a few had experience starting organizations.

This made getting started easier, but built in a few problems. In retrospect, it might have made sense to include some totally new voices. We thought we were all in agreement on the mission (wrong!) and on the WBC's goals (wrong again!).

The idea is to build a board thoughtfully, rather than to just let it happen. Efficient boards are contentious; inefficient boards can easily become rubber stamps for the one or two strongest voices.

## First Meeting of the Board of Directors

The first meeting of the board is critical for incorporating the organization and securing 501(c)(3) tax status.

Here's a suggested agenda:

▶ *Approve articles and bylaws.* Articles and bylaws are legal documents that define the organization and establish how it will be governed. Most of it is boilerplate. Do not do this yourself. Have a lawyer do it; he or she will do a better, faster, more accurate job than you can.

▶ *Elect officers.* You need at least a chair, a treasurer, and a secretary.

▶ *Authorize 501(c)(3) application.* This involves filling out IRS Form 1023, "Application for Recognition of Exemption Under Section 501(c)(3) of the Internal Revenue Code." Once more, have your lawyer do this. Yes, you can do it yourself—but why bother? You will have to walk through it with your lawyer and understand it. The filing fee depends on the donations you anticipate: $200 for under $25,000 a year, $500 for over $25,000.

▶ *Set meeting schedules.* Most boards will meet once a month, though at the beginning it may be necessary to meet more frequently.

▶ *Establish committees.* Standing committees, most notably finance, structure the work of the board. Early on, committees often do the administrative work, freeing the employees to work on the mission.

▶ *Appoint people to committees.* If all members are involved, the work will be lighter. Try to avoid appointing anyone who would do nothing more than lend his or her name to your masthead.

▶ *Authorize appropriate insurance coverage* (directors' and officers', general liability). Astute board members will ask for this coverage.

# Recruit Board Members

Maintain the list of possible board members and add to it or subtract from it as conditions change. Your criteria will shift over time. You will experience turnover—board members move, retire, find other interests, develop health problems, realize that they are overcommitted. Recruitment is an ongoing task for the board.

Recruitment begins with common-sense preparation. Put together a recruitment package that contains (at the very least) a list of current board members and key staff, board committees, a clear statement of the mission, the most recent annual report, newsletters or other publicity, and a schedule of board meetings. Add a job description for board members. What are their duties? How many hours per month will they be expected to serve? What will their responsibilities be for fundraising? Don't make the mistake of assuming that the prospect knows about the organization in any detail. You can always shorten a presentation.

Then set up meetings with prospective board members. Start with short informational sessions to sound out their interest in the organization and its mission. Do not plan to make an offer during this first meeting. You may find that the prospect is not interested, is currently overcommitted but would like to be considered later, is interested but is in some way not qualified. A common disqualifier: the probability of personality conflicts with current board members and staff. A small organization can't afford to deal with discord it could prevent.

If the prospect is suitable and if the nominating committee (or executive committee) agrees, then a more formal meeting is in order. Have a board member and the executive director meet with the prospect (breakfast or lunch meetings are not amiss) to ask him or her to join the board. This is the best chance you will get to make sure there are no substantial misunderstandings about the role of the board. Make it very clear that board membership is not just dressing for a resume (an all too common problem) but that it requires a high level of commitment and active participation in running the organization. Go over the board job description just to make sure that all parties understand what is involved. Assuming that the prospect is a good addition to the board, invite him or her to join, subject to board approval, as outlined in the bylaws.

*Make it very clear that board membership is not just dressing for a resume but that it requires a high level of commitment and active participation in running the organization.*

## Orient and Train New Board Members

Provide each new board member with a "director kit" that contains information about what the organization is doing and has been doing. Include information on the mission, bylaws, recent meeting minutes, copies of financial statements, the calendar of events, and perhaps program descriptions.

Introduce the new board member to both the board and the staff. Walk him or her through the facilities.

## Job Description for Board Member

1. Regularly attends board meetings and important related meetings.
2. Makes serious commitment to participate actively in committee work.
3. Volunteers for and willingly accepts assignments and completes them thoroughly and on time.
4. Stays informed about committee matters, prepares well for meetings, and reviews and comments on minutes and reports.
5. Gets to know other committee members and builds a collegial working relationship that contributes to consensus.
6. Participates actively in the committee's annual evaluation and planning efforts.
7. Participates in fundraising for the organization.

Good board members are made, not born. And since each nonprofit is in some sense unique, train even experienced board members. Training may be as structured as coursework with readings and other material or as simple as linking new board members with old board members. The idea is to help the new member feel at home and discover where his or her skills can best be employed as quickly as possible. This is yet another opportunity to make sure that the board members are unified and informed.

## Board Terms

How long should a board member's term be? How many consecutive years should a member serve? Should former board members be invited to join the board again? If so, how long should they be off the board before rejoining it?

There are no hard-and-fast rules here. Term limits are intended to provide a smooth turnover of the board. Scheduled turnover is intended to prevent board stagnation or ossification: boards that don't turn over tend to freeze in predictable patterns. For a gradual turnover, start with staggered terms: one, two, or three years.

Three years with one renewal (total of six consecutive years) is common. This allows for some continuity but builds in turnover. Board members who are superannuated can always choose to remain actively involved on committees and advisory boards, though even then they may be well advised to take a sabbatical to refresh. A good rule of thumb is that a board member should take a break from board duties for at least one full term (in this example, three years) in order to rekindle his or her enthusiasm and develop new ideas.

# Professional Advisors

You need a competent lawyer, accountant, insurance agent, and banker. You'll have plenty to do without attempting to be your own lawyer and accountant. (Anyway, only fools have themselves for clients.) Shop around for these professionals. Pick the ones with whom you feel most comfortable.

Consider using a marketing or public relations consultant. Once your advertising and marketing efforts become fairly routine, you might economize (though if you have capable advisors you won't want to), but to make sure that you start out on the right foot, hire experts. You might have the expertise on your board of directors.

Consultants (including the free or low-cost ones already mentioned) serve a variety of functions. The most important come from their depth of experience. They can save you time, money, and misspent effort. For example, a fundraising consultant with ten years' experience will have planned scores of fundraising campaigns, monitored their progress, and made constant improvements. That experience can make all the difference for your nonprofit. True, consultants cost a lot on a per-diem basis. But you are buying their training and experience, not just their time on task.

# Set up Bookkeeping, Accounting, and Office Systems

The first step toward getting the operating information you will need to run your organization is to make sure that you have the right kind of bookkeeping system.

You have a wide range of choices in bookkeeping and accounting systems. Some are low-cost, but demand a lot of your time. Most executive directors don't want to spend a lot of time being the bookkeeper and prefer to hire someone part-time. This is a choice that calls for professional advice. You want your systems to provide accurate, timely information in a format that will help you better manage your organization. You don't have to become a CPA, but you should be familiar enough with standard financial accounting practices to be able to read and use a balance sheet, an income statement, and a cash flow budget. (There is more on these in Chapter 6.)

*The first step toward getting the operating information you will need to run your organization is to make sure that you have the right kind of bookkeeping system.*

## Customized Systems

Designed for your business by a CPA (certified public accountant), a double-entry system (credits and debits) makes it easy to spot errors. Some economic historians claim that the invention of double-entry bookkeeping was as important as the invention of the printing press to modern business. Don't worry about becoming an expert bookkeeper. Hire one instead, and your accountant will help you understand and interpret the results.

## Computerized Systems

You will need a computerized system. Ask your accountant which one would make the most sense for you. The good ones allow for a high degree of customization, fitting the needs of your nonprofit and building in flexibility for future needs.

Accurate, timely information is so important in running a nonprofit that trying to economize in this area is like trying to economize on water when your house is on fire. Get the best assistance you can afford. It'll be worth it. To paraphrase Peter Drucker, if you have to ask why you need an accountant, you aren't ready to go into business, and if you can't afford a good accountant, you don't have enough money to go into business.

*To paraphrase Peter Drucker, if you have to ask why you need an accountant, you aren't ready to go into business.*

# Estimate Your Personnel Needs

Your biggest expense will be salaries and related costs (FICA, benefits). For now, use your best guesses. Keep this simple.

When you open the doors and begin providing programs and services, how many employees will you need? How many outside helpers?

How much will you pay them? Your peers in the nonprofit world are the best source of pay information. You may be paying employees by the hour or per program, but for the sake of simplicity round it out to dollars per month. Outside helpers (consultants, for example) usually are paid per project. If you will be adding employees during the first three months, how much will this add to your payroll?

Take the total payroll for employees (but not for outside helpers) and add 35 percent to cover added costs (as in Figure 2-2).

In this example, an executive director and an administrative assistant are on board at the beginning of month one. A part-time program manager is added at the start of month two.

In similar fashion, estimate the monthly cost of outside helpers (as in Figure 2-3).

| Name of Position | Month 1 Salary | Month 2 Salary | Month 3 Salary | 3-Month Total |
|---|---|---|---|---|
| Executive Director | 4,500 | 4,500 | 4,500 | 13,500 |
| Admin Assistant | 2,000 | 2,000 | 2,000 | 6,000 |
| Program Director | | 1,200 | 1,200 | 2,400 |
| | | | | 0 |
| | | | | 0 |
| | | | | 0 |
| Total Salary | 6,500 | 7,700 | 7,700 | 21,900 |
| Payroll | 8,775 | 10,395 | 10,395 | 29,565 |

**Figure 2-2.** Example of payroll and related expense

| Job | Month 1 Fee | Month 2 Fee | Month 3 Fee | 3-Month Total |
|---|---|---|---|---|
| Trainer | 500 | | 500 | 1,000 |
| Marketing Expert | 250 | 250 | | 500 |
| | | | | |
| | | | | |
| | | | | |
| Total | 750 | 250 | 500 | 1,500 |

**Figure 2-3.** Example of costs for outside help

# Estimate Your Immediate Cash Needs

Starting any organization takes cash. You have to buy supplies and furniture and equipment, put down deposits for rent and utilities, pay licensing or other fees (such as the $250 filing fee for a small 501(c)(3)), and legal and accounting costs. You may try to minimize these costs by seeking donations of furniture and equipment, but other costs will creep in.

Start with the big items. Make a list and keep a dollar tab. Use a spreadsheet and set up something like the example in Figures 2-4, 2-5, and 2-6.

| Item | Amount |
|------|--------|
| Furniture | 600 |
| Computer | 1,400 |
| Software | 600 |
| Phone/Fax | 240 |
| Copier | 600 |
| Lighting | 800 |
| Total FF&E | 4,240 |

**Figure 2-4.** Example of cash needs for first quarter FF&E (Furniture, Fixtures, and Equipment)

| Item | Amount |
|------|--------|
| FF&E | 4,240 |
| Fitout Premises | 2,200 |
| Utilities Deposit | 200 |
| Legal and Accounting | 1,200 |
| Licenses, Permits, Fees | 450 |
| Promotion/Advertising | 600 |
| Total One-Time Costs | 8,890 |

**Figure 2-5.** Example of one-time costs

Almost every organization needs to have basic computer and telephone capacity. Start with decent computers (you can get great capacity for under $600) and up-to-date software. You might not need a copier or special lighting. You will need some furniture. Listing your FF&E is straightforward. You might already have most of the things you need. List them anyway. They will reappear as a portion of Fixed Assets on your balance sheet.

One-time costs are peculiar to start-ups. FF&E is one of these. You may have to paint or clean up your proposed location, build shelves, or move a wall. These are lumped together as "fit out premises." You have to calculate deposits, licenses, permits, and fees. Less obvious one-time costs include extra legal and accounting costs. (Filing for incorporation and 501(c)(3) status and setting up the books are examples.)

| Operating Costs | Month 1 | Month 2 | Month 3 | 3-Month Total |
|---|---|---|---|---|
| Salaries and Benefits | 8,775 | 10,395 | 10,395 | 29,565 |
| Outside Helpers | 750 | 250 | 500 | 1,500 |
| Rent | 600 | 600 | 600 | 1,800 |
| Telephone | 600 | 600 | 500 | 1,800 |
| Utilities | 150 | 150 | 150 | 450 |
| Insurance | 200 | 200 | 200 | 600 |
| Interest | | | | 0 |
| Loan Payments | | | | 0 |
| Legal and Accounting | | 100 | 100 | 200 |
| Miscellaneous | 100 | 100 | 100 | 300 |
| Other | 50 | 50 | 50 | 150 |
| Total Operating Costs | 11,225 | 12,445 | 12,695 | 36,365 |

**Figure 2-6.** Example showing total operating costs for 3 months

Once up and running, your NPO will have ongoing legal and accounting costs but they will be captured as operating expenses in the *statement of activities* (the nonprofit equivalent of a for-profit income statement). Less obvious costs include pre-start-up marketing and public relations efforts, such as a fundraising event or a cocktail party for potential friends and donors.

The next step is to estimate operating costs, those costs incurred simply to keep the doors open. These prominently include salaries and benefits, space costs (rent or mortgage plus utilities), insurance premiums, and loan payments. At this stage don't worry about more subtle costs. (You'll get a chance to worry about them later on, in Chapter 4.) The idea is to have a rough estimate of three months' operating costs. Since this is a projection, it will not be 100 percent accurate—but it should give a sense of the magnitude of the costs.

Now add up the one-time costs and add the operating costs for three months. In the example, $8,890 + $36,365 = $45,255. This total represents your immediate cash needs.

Now, before you panic, these are just preliminary numbers. Some of the costs may be trimmed; you may get used FF&E, postpone hires, do without. It's up to you.

*Less obvious costs include pre-start-up marketing and public relations efforts, such as a fundraising event or a cocktail party for potential friends and donors.*

## Expert Advice: Take a Business Course to Refresh Your Skills

There are so many business courses that your problem may be where to start. In no special order, look into courses in the following areas:

1. *Financial management.* These put bookkeeping and accounting information to work for you. You have to know how to read a balance sheet, a profit and loss (income statement), and cash flow budget. Ignoring financial management is a quick way to stunt your future.
2. *Marketing.* These include sales training, advertising, and other marketing skills. Marketing (the process of creating customers) is what business is all about. You can never learn too much about how to attract and retain customers.
3. *Personnel.* Hiring, managing, evaluating, and even firing personnel will probably be a constant challenge for you. Find out the basic practices. No need to reinvent them.
4. *Planning.* The SCORE pre-business workshops are a good example.
5. *Taxes.* Take an IRS tax seminar. The Internal Revenue Service puts on short, useful seminars for new or prospective business owners. These courses cover basic tax and recordkeeping requirements (many of which apply to you and your NPO).

One of the great pleasures of working in a small organization is that it requires constant learning. Success comes from a host of incremental improvements: do this better, do that better. You don't have to master everything. You do have to know enough to spot omissions, mistakes, or other problems.

What matters is the discipline. Lay out what you will probably have to spend first. Then seek intelligent ways to lower costs. You do this for your home. Doing the same in a nonprofit may be a bit more complex, but basically it amounts to this: you set a budget, look for ways to economize without sacrificing too much, and then act within that budget.

# Learning from Experience: Running Example

Experience is a great educator. The participants of the Papoutsy Seminar for Women Entrepreneurs requested more structure and, interestingly, more speakers.

The workshops of the first year were replaced by a more structured program: every woman would be required to write a complete business plan, including financial statements, and defend her plan before a panel of bankers and business owners. Instead of using a single teacher augmented sporadically by guest speakers, the syllabus was built around a combination of teachers, panels, and guest speakers.

At the end of the second year, one of the participants, a former train-the-trainer specialist for IBM, made a compelling case for having the speakers understand adult learning styles. As a result, a much more interactive format was developed, one in which lecturing was held to a minimum. I found this difficult, so I bought a kitchen timer and asked one of the participants to let me know whenever I spoke more than three minutes. This was fine; I modified my style and since I was now the glue holding the seminar together (i.e., I was there every Saturday), the participants were pleased with the change.

Over the second and third years, the board worked diligently with the participants, speakers, and others to refine the mission statement. We all had a growing sense that we could do more than merely run an annual seminar. The participants fell roughly into two camps: those exploring the idea of "maybe perhaps possibly" someday owning a business and those who were seriously interested in ownership as soon as possible. The two groups of participants were sufficiently diverse to cause a problem. We were going too fast for the former and too slowly for the latter and we were clearly not reaching women who already owned businesses.

We had a hard time figuring out the mission. Should we limit the seminars to women in the Seacoast (the 13 miles along the Atlantic Ocean between Massachusetts and Maine)? We had a lot of applicants from all over southern New Hampshire and southern Maine, as well as a smattering of women from Massachusetts. Should we expand the curriculum? Seek a new model?

Somewhere in this period, the idea of incorporating came up as a serious possibility. There were several reasons for this. Chris felt, with good reason, that he had launched the program successfully and that it was time for it to stand on its own. If we were to become a 501(c)(3), we would have more latitude to experiment with new and innovative programs to address the concerns that participants had expressed over the start-up years.

# Writing a Mission Statement: Running Example

We used the seven questions listed in Chapter 1 to write our first formal mission statement.

**1. What is our purpose?** We want to *help women make informed decisions* about owning their own businesses.

**2. What business are we in?** We *educate, encourage, and counsel* women who are interested in owning their own business.

**3. What problems do we want to address?** Lack of knowledge of the how-tos of entrepreneurship. As a side issue, provide a welcoming and supportive format for exploring those how-tos.

**4. What services will we provide?** Direct programs (seminars, workshops) and access to business expertise as needed. Some mentoring would be necessary, but we couldn't agree on what that meant.

**5. Who has these problems? (Who is our customer?)** Women who lacked formal business education and basic business skills.

**6. Where are they?** Not surprisingly, we found that most of the women we were attracting to the program came from a comfortably affluent pool. That became a subject of intense debate later.

**7. What do they want**—*not what do you want to provide but rather what do they want you to provide?* We asked. They wanted the classroom experience to be augmented by some kind of moral support. This evolved into a highly successful peer mentoring program.

The active verbs "help," "educate," "encourage," and "counsel" stand out. For a first cut at a formal mission statement, we came up with this:

> The WBC helps women make informed decisions about business ownership by educating, encouraging and counseling them in workshops and providing access to a team of business experts.

Not bad for a first cut. Our stakeholders reviewed this draft and made constructive comments about adding mentoring, providing a supportive environment, and reaching beyond our narrow geographical area.

HELP
HERE

# Chapter 3

# Managing People, Part 1

**W**HY IS PERSONNEL MANAGEMENT SO IMPORTANT TO YOUR NPO? Compensation (salaries, taxes, and benefits) will be your biggest expense. If you want to run your NPO efficiently, you have to start by looking closely at how well you manage your employees.

Let's say you have five employees and one of them is a dud. That's 20 percent of your work force. That dud interferes with everyone else, griping and slouching around, upsetting other workers and making them uneasy. Say their productivity is reduced by 25 percent—a conservative estimate when you have a troublemaker on staff. A 25-percent reduction in productivity per person, times four people, equals a fifth person. With this 20-percent reduction in productivity represented by this "fifth person" and the 20 percent represented by your dud, that makes 40 percent of your work force unproductive! In a nonprofit with 50 employees, that would mean 20 not performing—a condition that wouldn't be tolerated for a minute. Yet that situation is by no means unusual in small nonprofits.

You can successfully compete for good employees and retain them. Your small NPO has many advantages, starting with close working relationships and communication with your employees. Larger nonprofits have to carefully plan ways to approximate some of the benefits executive directors of small organizations take for granted or don't even notice at all. Among these benefits are the following:

- ▶ Growth opportunities for individuals
- ▶ Recognition of successes
- ▶ Achievement, in the company and in the community
- ▶ Participation in management and other work-related decisions
- ▶ Efforts to clearly and consistently communicate organizational goals and challenges

Put these benefits to work for your organization. Use the forms and checklists in the next few chapters. You may alter them to suit your needs, but they will be useless if you do not use them.

## Some Legal Requirements

State laws concerning employment practices vary, but as a rough rule of thumb you are obligated to treat all job applicants fairly and equitably regardless of their race, color, religion, sex, or national origin.

*Rational employers simply want to proceed with business, comply with the laws, and be legally protected.*

Rational employers simply want to proceed with business, comply with the laws, and be legally protected. Lawsuits, no matter how groundless, are increasingly popular, perhaps because there is a lot of confusion about what constitutes an employee's or an applicant's rights.

What can you do to protect yourself? For a start:

- ▶ Be familiar with the basic legal obligations you bear as an employer. Some of them are listed in Figure 3-1.

- ▶ Whenever you have any doubt, as in terminating or suspending an employee, do not hesitate to call your lawyer.

- ▶ Take advantage of the information available to you from the U.S. Department of Labor, the Wage and Hour Division of the U.S. Department of Labor, the National Labor Relations Board, the Equal Employment Opportunity Commission, state labor departments and human rights commissions, and the IRS. They have a wealth of information and advice for you and will show you how to comply with the regulations. For free.

- ▶ Don't try to sail too close to the laws. Many employers get into legal problems by being too smart: not withholding Social Security and income tax payments, ignoring minimum wage or overtime laws, or exercising personal prejudices.

▶ Keep accurate, dated, written records: for hiring and recruiting, for promotions and evaluations, for disciplining and terminating, and for otherwise dealing with problem employees. The burden of proof against charges of discrimination will be on you. Few defenses are stronger than well-documented evidence that you have made, and continue to make, a good faith effort to comply with the law.

| Obligation | Basic Requirements |
|---|---|
| Federal Income Taxes | • Get IRS Form SS-4 for employer's identification number.<br>• Give new employees or employees changing the number of exemptions a W-4 (Employee's Withholding Exemption Certificate).<br>• Deposit withheld taxes according to IRS schedule on IRS Form 501.<br>• File Federal Payroll Tax Returns, Form 941, each quarter.<br>• Give employees completed W-2 forms at end of the calendar year. |
| Social Security Taxes (FICA) | • Obtain employee's Social Security number and withhold required percentage of wages from paycheck; contribute equal amount; deposit and report on IRS Form 501 (see above). |
| Federal Unemployment Tax (FUTA) | • Contribute and deposit percentage of employee's wages as required.<br>• File IRS Form 940, Employer's Annual Federal Unemployment Tax Return, on or before January 31. |
| State Unemployment Tax | • Check with state authorities; ask your accountant.<br>• Varies from state to state, and from industry to industry. |
| State Unemployment Insurance | • Check with state authorities; ask your accountant. |
| Workers' Compensation | • Check with your insurance agent. You must provide your employees with insurance coverage for job-related injury or accidents.<br>• Coverage may be obtained from the state or from private plans approved by the state.<br>• Varies state to state and for workers in different occupational classes. |

**Figure 3-1.** Employer obligations (continued on next page)

| Obligation | Basic Requirements |
|---|---|
| Employee Benefits | • See Chapter 11; check with your accountant to make sure your pension plan complies with ERISA and subsequent legislation. |
| Federal Wage and Hours | • Pay minimum wage; time-and-a-half for more than 40 hours a week; comply with child labor regulations. Retain basic payroll records and documentation of time worked. |
| EEOC (Title VII) | • If you have 15 or more employees: "Treat applicants and employees fairly and equally regardless of race, color, religion, sex (including pregnancy), or national origin in all employment practices including hiring, firing, promotion, compensation, and other terms, privileges and conditions of employment." |
| Equal Pay Act of 1963 | • Equal pay for equal work for both men and women. |
| Age Discrimination | • Treat applicants and employees equally regardless of age. The law specifies the 40 to 70 age group. |
| Employer with Federal Contracts or Subcontracts | • Prohibits discrimination in employment on the basis of race, color, religion, sex, or national origin.<br>• Covered employees must take affirmative action to hire and promote protected groups, qualified handicapped people, Vietnam-era Veterans, and disabled veterans of all wars. |
| OSHA: Occupational Safety & Health Act | • Provide safe work place; comply with OSHA occupational health and safety standards. |
| Local Fire Department | • Ask your local fire department for a compliance check on exits, stairs, location of fire extinguishing equipment, and so on. |
| Employment Eligibility | • Verify employment eligibility on Form I-9 as required by Immigration and Naturalization Service. |
| Posting Requirements | Somewhere in your work place, you may have to post:<br>• Fair Labor Standards Act Title VII of the Civil Rights Act<br>• OSHA bulletins<br>• Office of Federal Contract Compliance equal opportunity regulations<br>• Payday schedule<br>• Safety and health regulations<br>• Workers' Compensation carrier notice<br>• Unemployment and disability carrier notice<br>• Holiday schedules |

**Figure 3-1.** Employer obligations (continued)

Some organizations are exempt from some of the requirements sketched in Figure 3-1—but don't assume that yours is one of them. Check it out with your lawyer. Check first and check periodically. Laws change. So does their interpretation.

The best defense is to comply with the laws and treat all employees fairly, equitably, and consistently. Use the Golden Rule as a guideline: Treat others as you would have others treat you. While it can't guarantee you against an oddball lawsuit (nothing can), it will go a long way toward showing good faith in your dealings with employees.

The principle of fairness asks that you treat all applicants and employees evenhandedly, play no favorites, establish clear and consistent policies, and communicate them to your employees. Fairness does not demand that you hire anyone who applies—you can and should be discriminating in your choice of employees and choose those persons you think are best matched to the requirements of the job.

Good personnel practices will help you get the right worker for the job, allow the workers to produce for you, and even help you discipline or fire unwilling employees. The law does not require you to be the employer of last resort.

*The principle of fairness asks that you treat all applicants and employees evenhandedly, play no favorites, establish clear and consistent policies, and communicate them to your employees.*

# Do I Need Another Employee?

The most basic rule for personnel management is "Never hire anyone without a good business reason." To do this, tie your personnel plan to your business plan, that is, to the overall goals that you set for your organization.

## Why Should You Write a Personnel Plan?

To prepare for change;

- ▶ To be ready to replace retiring employees;
- ▶ To prepare for other departing employees;
- ▶ To compete for—and retain—good employees;
- ▶ To avoid last-minute hires for critical jobs;
- ▶ To protect your cash flow; and
- ▶ To minimize fixed expenses.

- ▶ What personnel do you have now?
- ▶ What are they doing? Have their tasks been timed?
- ▶ Can their jobs be restructured to accommodate projected growth?
- ▶ Do you maintain a skills bank (a listing of the skills and training of your employees)?
- ▶ Can overtime be used to avoid hiring?
- ▶ If no overtime is currently being paid, why not?
- ▶ According to your business plan, what will your personnel needs be in six months? One year? Five years?
- ▶ What replacements do you foresee?
- ▶ What critical jobs might have to be filled?
- ▶ What is the replacement time—recruiting, orienting, training—for these jobs?

At least once a year, write down your answers to these questions for each critical position, including your own:

- ▶ What has to be done to replace _____?
- ▶ What lead times are needed?
- ▶ What training time is involved?
- ▶ Where would I find a replacement for _____?

Try to list at least five sources for personnel—perhaps your files, colleagues in other nonprofits, employment agencies, vocational schools, referrals from current employees. Then form a backup plan. The ideal replacement is hard to find; the longer you plan ahead, the better.

**Figure 3-2.** Personnel early planning questions

If you raise questions here that you can't answer, don't worry. That's the point of this exercise. Look for options now, when you aren't under the gun. Compare alternatives. Ask for advice from your peers in the nonprofit world, business owners, and even bankers.

## Succession Plan

The most important critical position is that of executive director (ED). Make sure that you have a succession plan that shows how the ED might be replaced. Can a current employee or even a board member fill the gap? Who will do the ED's work in the interim period it takes to recruit and hire a new ED? The quality of the ED is a major concern of funders, since most small NPOs are extensions of the ED's personality, and a succession plan helps alleviate their concerns.

# Early Planning: Listing Tasks

What tasks have to be done in your organization? Identify and list the ongoing tasks—open the door, turn on lights, get ready to welcome clients who come in, … turn out lights, close and lock the door…. You want to list these carefully so you can assign them to your employees.

Most tasks fall into one of four categories:

1. Daily
2. Weekly
3. Monthly
4. Occasionally

Use Figure 3-3 and jot down the tasks as they occur to you under the appropriate heading. It takes time to do this thoroughly. You will overlook some of the tasks the first few times through.

Some tasks will involve more than one person: one person can't handle the job alone, some cooperation and socializing on the job is important for employee morale, or the timetable demands cooperation. Sometimes the wisdom of "many hands make light work" does not apply: cooperation disrupts other tasks and wastes time.

Your aim in Figure 3-4 is to get a handle on those tasks that take more than one person. It isn't to squeeze 2,400 minutes of productive time out of each employee each week. A secondary aim is to help you establish norms for tasks and projects that get repeated periodically. You need norms—time records of how long a task should take—to improve productivity, prevent too much employee slack time, and run your organization efficiently.

*Sometimes the wisdom of "many hands make light work" does not apply: cooperation disrupts other tasks and wastes time.*

| Task | Daily | Weekly | Monthly | Other (Specify) |
|------|-------|--------|---------|-----------------|
|      |       |        |         |                 |
|      |       |        |         |                 |
|      |       |        |         |                 |
|      |       |        |         |                 |
|      |       |        |         |                 |
|      |       |        |         |                 |
|      |       |        |         |                 |

**Figure 3-3.** Task listing

| Name of Task: | | | |
|---|---|---|---|
| **Person** | **What He/She Does** | **Daily, Weekly, Monthly, Occasionally (Specify)** | **Hours** |
| | | | |
| | | | |
| | | | |
| | | | |
| | | | |
| | | | |
| | | | |
| | | | |
| **Comments** | | **Total Hours** | |
| | | | |

**Figure 3-4.** Form for large tasks

Do a form as in Figure 3-4 for each task or project that takes more than one person's time. You may want to set a criterion for the tasks or projects that you quantify, such as length (e.g., any task taking more than six hours) or frequency (any task occurring more than once a month), to limit the paperwork. Once you establish norms and improve performance, this management tool will be indispensable.

Collate times (roughly) by week and employee. Parkinson's Law, "Work expands to fill the time allotted," is especially hard on small organizations. You have to make sure that your employees spend their time (the NPO's money) productively. You cannot do that without knowing in detail how they spend their work hours—and how they should be spending them. You need facts, time, and more facts.

Use the information from Figures 3-3 and 3-4 to fill in Figure 3-5.

When you go over these sheets, keep asking:

▶ Who should do this job/task?

▶ Does he or she have enough time? Too much time?

▶ Could it be better scheduled?

▶ Does it have to be done at all?

You may find that another employee isn't needed, that you can reschedule and coordinate your current employees' efforts more productively. Or you may find that you do need to add another person—and now you have a well-defined set of tasks for that person to perform. Keep these lists of tasks. You will be able to use them later to create job descriptions.

Make sure you hire:

▶ Only for a clear need

▶ To increase cash flow

▶ To replace an employee whose presence was justified

▶ For planned growth

If you have any doubts, do not hire. Postpone the decision. Consider the alternatives:

▶ Get part-time help (including volunteers and interns)

▶ Contract the work out

▶ Use a temporary agency

▶ Use a consultant

## Hidden Costs of Volunteers and Interns

At first you may think that volunteers and interns automatically save you money—no or low salaries, no benefits! But consider the hidden costs of time for you or some other employee to train and monitor their performance. Add in the overhead costs (administrative and space and equipment). Then there is the impact of a new volunteer or intern on an already overburdened staff.

Nothing is free in the nonprofit world.

Fill out this form and have your employees fill them out for several weeks. A word or two is enough to describe how the time is being used.

# How Is Time Really Spent?

Your quickest management payoff comes when you budget time for management functions. A large business has specialists for each management function. In your organization, you have to fill the role of several specialists—maybe all of them.

| Name of Employee: | | | | | | |
|---|---|---|---|---|---|---|
| Time | Sat/Sun | Mon | Tue | Wed | Thur | Fri |
| 8:00 | | | | | | |
| 8:30 | | | | | | |
| 9:00 | | | | | | |
| 9:30 | | | | | | |
| 10:00 | | | | | | |
| 10:30 | | | | | | |
| 11:00 | | | | | | |
| 11:30 | | | | | | |
| 12:00 | | | | | | |
| 12:30 | | | | | | |
| 1:00 | | | | | | |
| 1:30 | | | | | | |
| 2:00 | | | | | | |
| 2:30 | | | | | | |
| 3:00 | | | | | | |
| 3:30 | | | | | | |
| 4:00 | | | | | | |
| 4:30 | | | | | | |
| 5:00 | | | | | | |
| 5:30 | | | | | | |
| 6:00 | | | | | | |

**Figure 3-5.** Form for employee time use

Use Figure 3-6 and the section "The Managerial Functions" to make sure that each area is covered. A smoothly running organization is one where all of these functions are covered, not brilliantly perhaps, but adequately.

Make sure that each area is assigned to an individual. That person—you or a colleague—should then examine how the time is actually being used. Keep a time diary (such as Figure 3-5) to track how you spend your time.

Otherwise, you can become more efficient only by chance.

| Task | Person Responsible | Hours/Week | | Hours/Month | |
|---|---|---|---|---|---|
| | | Actual | Proposed | Actual | Proposed |
| Planning | | | | | |
| Organizing | | | | | |
| Staffing | | | | | |
| Supervising | | | | | |
| Directing | | | | | |
| Controlling | | | | | |
| Innovating | | | | | |
| | | | | | |

**Figure 3-6**. Managerial worksheet

Compare the results of Figure 3-6 and the structure of your organization. If you don't have an organization chart, make one.

A simple organization chart (Figure 3-7) for a small NPO might include the positions shown in Figure 3-7.

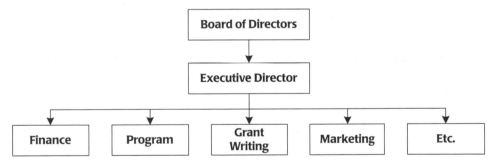

**Figure 3-7**. Standard organization chart

Make sure that no major position is left uncovered. A single person—you—may be filling all of these positions or you may be sharing or delegating duties. Some individual, whether you or a trusted employee, has to be responsible for each of these duties. A job assigned to everybody (or assigned by default) is a job assigned to nobody—and a job that won't get done. That kind of omission murders small NPOs.

Top management (you) has duties above and beyond those shown in Figure 3-7 and below under "The Managerial Functions." New business development, public relations and advertising, succession planning, and setting long-term goals are duties that don't fit into most charts.

# The Managerial Functions

### 1. Planning

- ▶ Set objectives.
- ▶ Establish strategies to attain objectives.
- ▶ Set benchmarks to measure progress.
- ▶ Choose tactics to make the strategies effective; make action plans.
- ▶ Determine resources needed: capital, equipment, facilities, personnel.
- ▶ Allocate resources.
- ▶ Create special plans, including financial, marketing, and personnel.

Basic questions:

- ▶ Where is the organization going in the next three years?
- ▶ What challenges and opportunities do you face?
- ▶ What resources do you have—and what do you lack?
- ▶ What programs or services do you want to start or to abandon?

### 2. Organizing

Work backwards from the organization's objectives and forward from the present. Determine:

- ▶ What tasks have to be done?
- ▶ When?
- ▶ By whom?
- ▶ With what resources?

### 3. Staffing

- ▶ Assign the right person to the right job.
- ▶ Make sure that someone is available for each necessary task.
- ▶ Project short-term needs (one or two years) and long-term needs (two to four years).

Avoid the ad-hoc staffing prevalent in small organizations—"This has to be done! Quick, get someone here to do it or I'll do it myself …."

### 4. Supervising

- ▶ Observe your employees and ensure that they are performing their duties effectively.
- ▶ Train to make sure skills are up to the tasks.
- ▶ Upgrade the responsibilities of good employees whenever possible, in order to retain them.

Your employees are adults who need little supervision, but they need some guidance and coordinating or productivity will slip and performance evaluations become impossible.

### 5. Directing

If routines are impaired or disrupted, decisions about what to do have to be made. Ideally, this is rare.

However, many managers spend far more time directing than makes good business sense, because it's very gratifying to put out fires. Let your employees direct their own work as much as possible; it helps them develop and perform better and it enables you to spend your time more effectively.

### 6. Controlling

For the basic control systems—operations, financial, accounting and book-keeping, personnel management:

- ▶ Gather timely, factual information routinely.
- ▶ Analyze information for deviations from the norms set in your planning and managing efforts.

### 7. Coordinating

Making all the parts and people in an organization work in concert toward common goals is a task worthy of a maestro. Marketing and finance have to harmonize; fundraising and ongoing programs need to keep the same time. Think of the maestro conducting the orchestra: coordinating, timing, scheduling, prompting, and keeping all performers focused on the same score.

### 8. Innovating

Allocate time to think about the future of your organization. Do not leave it to chance. What new products, new technologies, and new ideas will affect your organization in the next several years?

People who look for opportunities find opportunities. It's a management responsibility.

*Making all the parts and people in an organization work in concert toward common goals is a task worthy of a maestro.*

49

| Day/Time | Seek Opportunities | Plan | Organize | Measure | Improve |
|---|---|---|---|---|---|
| Monday | | | | | |
| Tuesday | | | | | |
| Wednesday | | | | | |
| Thursday | | | | | |
| Friday | | | | | |
| Saturday/Sunday | | | | | |

**Figure 3-8.** Daily management tasks—scheduling all major management functions

# Time and Task Analysis

What tasks are being performed now, by whom, and when?

Return to Figures 3-2, 3-3, and 3-4. Reexamine them, observe your employees' actual performance, and get actual times.

This is not a judgmental step. Don't look to improve any particular task at this stage. Some can be improved, some will not be worth doing, and others will be done about as well as possible. Solicit your employees' advice. Most employees want to do their jobs well, but if the jobs have been poorly planned or coordinated (your fault, not theirs), their zeal can't compensate.

What you want is a simple narrative:

First, I set up the clinic. That takes an hour. Then I review the client list for the day. Ten, 15 minutes. Provide services for two and a half hours. Coffee break in there somewhere—15 minutes. Lunch. One hour. Set up for the afternoon and check supplies. Half hour. Provide services for three hours. Coffee break, 15 minutes. Shut down and clean up. Twenty minutes or so.

You could get more details if you want, but this would be enough to start with.

Your employees are full of ideas and information about their jobs—how to improve them, change them, speed them up. Think of jobs you've had in the past: if you had one where the boss wanted your input, it was a good job, while if the boss dictated what you could do and when, it was a lousy job.

You can help your employees with Figure 3-9, Task Analysis, by gently directing them: "When you get here, what do you do first? Then what? ... I see. Then? ..." and so on. If there are more than ten tasks, use another sheet. At this stage you should begin to examine each job for improvements or changes. A good rule of thumb is "If a practice has remained unchanged for a year, it's out of date and needs to be re-examined."

| Position: | Date: | | |
|---|---|---|---|
| Task | Time Spent Now | Suggested Revisions | Estimated Revised Time |
| 1. | | | |
| 2. | | | |
| 3. | | | |
| 4. | | | |
| 5. | | | |
| 6. | | | |
| 7. | | | |
| 8. | | | |
| 9. | | | |
| 10. | | | |

**Figure 3-9.** Task analysis

## Improving Time Use

You need a calendar (large, with lots of room for writing), a supply of Weekly Time Planning Schedules (Figure 3-10), and a daily things-to-do list. Most time management systems are extrapolations on these simple tools.

The idea is to concentrate on the most important—not necessarily the most pressing—tasks. What do you want to accomplish in the next quarter or six months? That's where the calendar helps. Set down your goals. Then work backwards to identify those tasks you have to perform to reach those goals.

Now break the tasks down into the Weekly Time Planning Schedule format. List the problems and/or objectives for each week. Keep the list short. Half a dozen problems or objectives a week is enough for anyone. This helps establish priorities; the undone list at the end of the week tends to get attention.

A daily things-to-do list breaks the larger jobs into manageable bits, ensures that appointments are kept, and provides a helpful record of what you did (and when) for IRS and other purposes. The daily entries should be

| Name: _____ | Week Ending: _____ | |
|---|---|---|
| **Problems/Objectives** | **Schedule** | |
| | Monday | |
| | Tuesday | |
| | Wednesday | |
| | Thursday | |
| | Friday | |
| | Saturday | |
| | Sunday | |

**Figure 3-10.** Weekly time planning schedule

related to the problems and objectives for the week—a handy check on what you do first.

Your input makes these forms valuable. They can give you a lot of information, especially in retrospect when you see what tasks you postponed or let slide. They help you spend your time more profitably if you use them.

## What Should Be Done—and by Whom?

*T*he time management puzzle is almost solved and you're closer to a definitive answer to that big question, "Do you need another employee?"

The time management puzzle is almost solved and you're closer to a definitive answer to that big question, "Do you need another employee?" After listing and timing all the major jobs in your company, ask of each one, "*Why do this task at all?*"

If you come up with at least one good answer to that question, here are some other questions to ask:

▶ Who is doing this?

▶ When? Where? How?

▶ Could someone else do it better?

▶ How can it be done better? (Organizing, coordinating, staffing? New equipment? Training? Farm it out? ...)

▶ How do other nonprofits handle this job? (You can always learn from your peers.)

Look for big improvements first. Delete a task, combine it with another job, reorganize, reschedule, or simplify it to gain a big improvement.

The same goes for your own time use. Many EDs open the mail, balance the checkbook, run errands to "spare the secretary," and ignore management tasks. Ask yourself the tough questions: Who should be doing this—me or someone else? When? Why do it at all?

## Do You Still Need Another Employee?

Match up the information you have assembled with the resources and people available.

For each employee, check again how his or her time is actually being used. Is there extra time available? When? Are the employee's skills appropriate to the tasks?

If all employees are working up to capacity and there's slack time left, fine. Too tight a schedule leads to anger, frustration, and sloppy work.

However, the same is true for too loose a schedule. Better pay some overtime than have a bunch of bored, underemployed employees collecting weekly paychecks. No overtime indicates overstaffing.

▶ Which tasks need more time?

▶ Do a lot of jobs have to be done over? For better quality, do it right the first time.

▶ Are there new tasks to be done?

▶ Is the change temporary or permanent?

Now, do you still need to hire?

If yes, begin working on the job description and start recruiting. Otherwise, sit tight. When paying overtime begins to hurt or your current employees call for help, then repeat the process.

HELP
HERE

# Chapter 4

# Managing People, Part 2

THINK OF A MANAGER ASSEMBLING A BASEBALL TEAM. YOUR JOB IS similar—to get the right kind of performance from your organization, you have to staff it correctly and match the requirements of the job with the skills and abilities of your employees.

If you get the right players for the positions, your job is greatly simplified. Get the wrong ones and performance is going to suffer.

Think of the baseball team. If you need a first baseman, you'd start by thinking of what a player in that position does. Next, what skills and abilities does the position require? What are the most desirable characteristics of a first baseman? Among other things, sure are needed hands for catching the ball and fielding and a proven ability to hit curve balls with power. Other preferred characteristics include being tall, left-handed, and "coachable."

The same kind of process applies to staffing an NPO. You don't have room for error, so plan ahead. The Employee Planning Form (Figure 4-1) is a good starting point.

# Job Descriptions

## The Job Description Process

**Step 1.** Fill out Figure 4-1 for each position, actual or contemplated. This will help you (and your employee) to better understand just what the job involves and how much time each task takes, and lay the basis for a realistic job description, time-use improvement, productivity gains, and performance evaluations, and even provide legally helpful information.

If your NPO is small enough, you may want to simply list every single activity you can think of on this form and then arrange them into logical jobs. In any case, first list all of the activities you can think of; then go back and estimate the amount of time each activity should take.

| Task/Function | Estimated Time | Comments |
|---|---|---|
| 1. | | |
| 2. | | |
| 3. | | |
| 4. | | |
| 5. | | |
| 6. | | |
| 7. | | |
| 8. | | |
| 9. | | |
| 10. | | |
| 11. | | |
| 12. | | |
| 13. | | |
| 14. | | |
| 15. | | |
| 16. | | |
| 17. | | |
| 18. | | |
| 19. | | |
| 20. | | |
| Total Time | | |

**Figure 4-1.** Employee planning form

**Step 2.** Review the preliminary Employee Planning Form with your employees. They will spot omissions and errors and offer helpful comments. Your employees are your best single source of information about operations in your business. Put their expertise to work for you.

Once you have reviewed the form and made corrections, put it aside for a day or two. Other insights may come along.

**Step 3.** Add up all the times. You may find that the total is excessive. Maybe some of the jobs are done concurrently, or are not necessary, or can be scheduled better, or can be done by someone else.

Keep your overall objectives in mind: to improve your organization, to create realistic job descriptions, and to make very sure that you don't add unnecessary employees. This is where the Comments section is especially helpful—jot down the ideas as they come along so you don't lose them. Ask, ask again, and listen.

**Step 4.** Begin the job description, Figure 4-2. If you already have job descriptions for each position, now is the time to compare each job description with what is actually being done to make sure that you don't miss any important function.

### Keeping Job Descriptions Current

Job descriptions make replacing an employee much simpler—the job requirements are available, so the search for a replacement can start quickly. And since jobs change, another reason to maintain up-to-date job descriptions is to make sure there is no serious dislocation between the job description and the real world.

For every job, ask:

▶ Is this job necessary?

▶ Can it be done by somebody else?

▶ Can it be done somewhere else? In a better way? At a better time?

▶ Has this job/position been reviewed recently? When?

*Seize every opportunity to question the need for each job slot. You can't afford to carry dead weight.*

Seize every opportunity to question the need for each job slot. You can't afford to carry dead weight. If you aren't paying overtime now and again, worry. Lack of overtime always signifies overstaffing.

**Step 5.** Start at the beginning of the Job Description Form. What's the title of the new job? Who is preparing the form? When?

| Position:_____ |
| Date Prepared:_____ |
| By:_____ |

| Task/Function | Estimated Hours per Week | Job Description: |
|---|---|---|
| 1. | | |
| 2. | | |
| 3. | | |
| 4. | | |
| 5. | | |
| 6. | | |
| 7. | | |
| 8. | | |
| 9. | | |
| 10. | | |
| | | Job Specifications: |

**Figure 4-2.** Job description

Now fill in the functions and times. (Use Figure 4-1, Employee Planning Form, for each job.) Add up the times—most employees don't want to work 80-hour weeks. If the job is unrealistic, change the job. It's a lot easier to change a job than to change a person.

As you fill in the functions, keep notes on what skills, formal training, licensing, aptitude, and experience are necessary or ideal for the job. You can always relax standards to get the right person or a person who would be ideal with a bit more training. Skills and qualifications must be job-related to avoid legal problems. If you have any question at all about whether or not your hiring practices are legal, check with your lawyer.

Once you know what the specs are and what the job involves, the hardest part of writing the job description is over. A job description in small organizations may have to be updated frequently until routines become established, but it's easier than making the first version. Remember: for each job, you must list key functions and establish norms.

There's an important principle involved here: Everyone needs to know what he or she is responsible for, even if the responsibilities are only sketched in. You will use the job descriptions for evaluating personnel, for promotions and salary reviews, and for improving your business operations.

Most of all, you will use them to communicate clearly with your employees and to ensure that the duties and responsibilities of each job are understood.

**Step 6.** Finish the job description. Write a brief synopsis of the duties, note the person to whom the employee reports, and review and list the job specifications. For a highly regimented job, the list of functions tends to be longer than for a job with considerable autonomy. Your duties include some vague ones—planning, motivating, innovating—while a custodial job might include sweeping the sidewalks, washing windows, changing lightbulbs, and stocking shelves.

The job description and list of job specifications in the example (appendix at end of chapter, page 82) were used in the advertisement for the position, as a way to clarify what the job involved and as a preliminary screening tool. Note that the job specifications clearly pertain to the position. All the basic questions an applicant might reasonably ask are addressed—salary, basic skills, and experience needed.

No job description is complete without noting that it is not an implied contract or job offer for applicants nor is it ironclad and proof against change as circumstances warrant.

## Who Needs Job Descriptions?

Use job descriptions for all current employees, volunteers, and interns, especially if you haven't been using job descriptions as a management tool. "Current employees" includes you. Volunteers have to know who they report to, what they are expected to do, schedules, and so on. Interns need more direct hands-on management, but that begins with a clear job description.

## Volunteers

Job descriptions are needed for all employees, especially volunteers. Volunteers need to be told clearly what their job involves, when the duties are to be performed, to whom they report, and when and how their performance will be reviewed. Treat your volunteers with respect and provide them opportunities to grow and learn new skills. You and they will both benefit.

The sentences at the bottom of the job description are there for a purpose. "We reserve the right to change or revise duties and responsibilities as the need arises. This document is not a written or implied contract of employment." If you create your own form, include these words—they may save you legal headaches.

# How Do I Get Good Employees?

If I had known then what I know now, would I have hired the same people? How would I change my choices if I could turn back the clock?

Finding the right person calls for having information about the applicants, from their application forms, interviews, tests, and reference checks. Armed with this information, you can discriminate between those persons you think will work and those persons you suspect might not. You cannot legally discriminate on the basis of sex, religion, creed, national origin, handicaps, or age. But the law doesn't imply that you can't select the best applicant from those you interview, nor does it compel you to hire anyone if you don't find the right person.

Where do you find people with the right skills and attitudes? By hiring intelligently from a pool of qualified applicants. If you have only one candidate, you run an enormous risk and limit your choices.

Start with the job description. While you may be tempted to alter it to fit an attractive candidate, keep in mind that the reason you developed a job description was to ensure that certain functions are performed. The job description will help whether you advertise the job inside your organization (a shot at a promotion is a great morale builder) or you advertise outside, through either a newspaper or an employment agency.

Selecting the best person for the job makes good sense. If you find that person inside your organization, great. If not, that's OK too; by bringing in an outsider you also bring in fresh ideas and insights. A policy of always promoting from within is as stultifying as never promoting from within. Hire the best person available.

*Finding the right person calls for having information about the applicants, from their application forms, interviews, tests, and reference checks.*

# Form a Pool

Get a number of qualified applicants from which to select. This may seem impossible at times, especially in a crowded labor market, but there are at least a dozen sources. See Figure 4-3 for their positive and negative points.

| Source | Advantages/Disadvantages | Comments |
|---|---|---|
| 1. Current Employees | You know their strengths and weaknesses. Promoting from within provides a chance for them to grow. But look out for favoritism, lack of new ways of doing things, and promoting an unqualified but senior person. | You must consider current employees first, for the sake of employee morale. |
| 2. Former Employees | Same as above. | Consider retired workers for part-time work. |
| 3. Employee Referrals | Recruitment costs are low, and these people can easily fit into your work force. But watch out for nepotism and formation of cliques. Lowered morale can follow if referral is not hired. | Stress that you will hire the best, most qualified candidate. |
| 4. Advertising | Your ad can reach a large number of people, and can aim at a target group via specific media. But you may get too many unqualified applicants. | Make your ad specific, and base it on the job description to avoid attracting weak candidates. |
| 5. Schools, Colleges, etc. | Recruitment costs are low, and the school may screen candidates for you. Tradeoff: enthusiasm for experience. | Many schools have active placement services. Make yourself known to them. |
| 6. Private Employment Agencies | These agencies will work for you, and will interview and screen candidates for you. But they are the most expensive short-term alternative. | The best solution for hard-to-fill jobs. Long-term, the least expensive alternative. |

**Figure 4-3.** Sources of applicants (continued on next page)

| Source | Advantages/Disadvantages | Comments |
|---|---|---|
| 7. Public Employment Agencies | These agencies don't charge, and they provide excellent testing, job analysis, and indexing services. They will work with you and for you if they know your needs. But they may send unqualified or unmotivated applicants. | Get to know the local agency employees. |
| 8. Disabled Workers | These people are highly motivated, and tend to have low absenteeism. Service agencies will often help train them. But you may have insurance and facility access problems. | Involve present employees to help overcome their resistance. |
| 9. Professional Societies | These societies have low or no fees, but their resources are limited. | Good source of professionals or managers. |
| 10. Labor Unions | Unions have no fees and may provide a number of qualified applicants. But they may not send you their best applicants. | Good for skilled craft positions, e.g., electricians. |
| 11. Walk-ins | Their recruitment doesn't cost you anything, and they are interested in working for you. But they are an unstable source. | Make a file of these people's skills for future reference. |
| 12. Friends and Relations | They know and like you, and may know the NPO well. But they may expect special treatment. | Ever fire a friend? However, they may be the only source in a startup or marginal NPO. |
| 13. Other NPOs | No cost, may be a good source of candidates. But: raiding another NPO will backfire. | Call and ask. Transfers between nonprofits are common. |
| 14. Chamber of Commerce | No cost; may have knowledge of qualified administrative or managerial people new to your area. | Worth calling |

**Figure 4-3.** Sources of applicants (continued)

Of the various ways to find a pool of qualified applicants, the least expensive in the long run is the most costly upfront: specialized employment agencies for the most skilled and/or important positions, followed by other employment agencies (including government agencies). Since the cost of a bad hire is so large—look at the disruption and bad feelings alone, if wasted time and salary don't make the point clearly enough—the cost of using an employment agency is less than it appears. Depending on the job, the employment agency charge will range from 10 percent to 30 percent or more of the employee's first year's salary.

Publicize your search. Your advertisement—whether internal (bulletin board or direct communication with your employees) or external (employment agencies, institutions, newspapers, or trade bulletins)—should be based on the job description you have carefully drawn up.

Begin your search inside your organization. While you may not find the right person, the attention and possibility of a promotion boosts morale. If training could make an employee ready for a promotion, consider it carefully.

*Begin your search inside your organization. While you may not find the right person, the attention and possibility of a promotion boosts morale.*

## Gather Applications

Have all applicants fill out an application. A legal application form is provided below (Figure 4-4, Employee Application Form). You may want to get a more specialized form—ask the United Way or an employment agency. The information the application form provides helps you make a sensible hiring decision.

**Employee Application Form (Please Print)**

Name _____ Social Security Number _____

Street Address _____ Apt No. _____

City _____ State _____ ZIP _____

Telephone Number _____ E-Mail _____

Date of Birth _____

How did you hear about the job? _____

_____

**Figure 4-4.** Employee application form (continued on next page)

School most recently attended:

Name _____ Location _____ Phone _____

Graduated? Yes ____ No ____ Now enrolled? Yes ____ No ____

Last grade completed? _____

Major _____

---

Physical

Any health problems or physical defects that could affect your employment?

Yes ____ No ____

If yes, please explain _____

_____

During the past 10 years, have you ever been convicted of a crime, excluding misdemeanors and traffic violations? Yes ____ No ____

If yes, please explain in full _____

_____

---

Personal references (other than family):

Name _____ Telephone number _____

Name _____ Telephone number _____

Name _____ Telephone number _____

Interviewer or reference comments: _____

_____

_____

---

This section to be filled out by employer only after hire:

Job title _____ Hourly rate or salary _____

Start date_____

Tax status _____ Number of exemptions _____

Person to contact in case of emergency

Name _____

**Figure 4-4.** Employee application form (continued on next page)

1. I certify that the information contained in this application is correct to the best of my knowledge and understand that deliberate falsification of this information is grounds for dismissal.
2. I authorize the references listed above to give you any and all information concerning my previous employment and pertinent information they may have, personal or otherwise, and release all parties from all liability for any damage that may result from furnishing same to you.
3. I acknowledge that if I become employed, I will be free to resign at any time for any reason, and that management similarly reserves the right to terminate my employment at will.

Date _____  Signature _____

**Figure 4-4.** Employee application form (continued)

## Cull the Applicants

You want to choose the best candidate from a number of qualified applicants, but unless you're a masochist, you don't want to interview everyone remotely interested in the job.

Those applicants who don't meet the job specs may be fine for another job. File their applications for future reference. Usually it's easy to weed out applicants, such as those who want more money than the job is worth.

Now go through the applications of those who apparently meet the job requirements. These are the ones to interview. If the number is unwieldy, look for other ways to reduce the pool. Look for gaps in their applications and seek clarification.

After you've weeded out as many as possible, check the references of those remaining. If you don't have three candidates left, recruit some more—you owe yourself a good selection.

Reference checks are tricky. An applicant who is refused a job on the basis of a reference is legally entitled to a copy of the reference, so many people won't give you negative information. This puts the person giving the reference in an awkward spot—so be careful.

When checking references, look for facts: dates of graduation, employment dates, and other factual information. In the sidebar are some questions that can help you make a decision.

Your aim is to get the reference to talk. You can always ask him or her to comment further, but don't be surprised if some references choose not to comment. (Note that "I'd rather not comment on that" is a particularly revealing comment!)

*When checking references, look for facts: dates of graduation, employment dates, and other factual information.*

## Can-Do and Will-Do Questions

**"Can-Do" Questions:**

1. Did he/she work for you as a _____?
2. Did he/she perform to your satisfaction?
3. What did he/she do well?
4. What did he/she do poorly?
5. Would you rehire him/her?
6. Why or why not?

**"Will-Do" Questions:**

1. He/she says he/she left your company because _____ Could you tell me more about that?
2. Would you rate his/her attendance as average, below average, or above average?
3. Did he/she get along well with customers and fellow workers?
4. Did he/she respond well to close supervision on the job?

Sometimes you will receive such a glowing reference that the essentially negative function of reference checking is overlooked. If you have an applicant who is heartily endorsed by more than one reference, you may have a gem. Check anyway; the rule on references is L.I.A.R.: *Look Into All References*.

Keep the applications of those you don't wish to consider further; let them know that you want to keep their applications on hand for future recruitment. Then, interview the remaining applicants.

**I. Define the interview's purpose beforehand:**

▶ Determine ability to do the job.
▶ Determine willingness to do the job.

**II. Procedure:**

▶ Review application, check references before the interview.
▶ Relax applicant.
▶ Describe job as thoroughly as possible.
▶ Give applicant a copy of job description.
▶ Ask questions about prior employment: dates, duties, locations.
▶ Ask about likes, dislikes, reasons for leaving jobs, preferred kinds of supervision and working conditions.
▶ Ask about applicant's expectations for job. Look for fits and mismatches

**Figure 4-5.** Interviewer's guidelines (continued on next page)

with job realities (money, hours, opportunities for growth and advancement, job security, and so on).

▶ Give information about policies, working conditions, advantages of working for your company, your own expectations for prospective employee. (If you were to present this information sooner, you'd get back an echo: what the applicant thinks you want to hear.)

▶ Give applicant your time frame for hiring decision.

▶ Do not hire on the spot. Check references further. Get results of physical and skill tests, if indicated.

**III. Follow-up:**

After applicant leaves, jot down impressions, questions you wished you had asked, and thoughts for following up in a further interview. Use Figure 4-9, Selection Summary Sheet.

**Figure 4-5.** Interviewer's guidelines (continued)

If you decide not to include an applicant in a second round of interviews, tell him or her, explaining only that you're interviewing applicants who better match the requirements of the job. The reason to choose one candidate over another is always that the one is a better match for the job requirements, even if part of the reason is an adverse reference.

*The reason to choose one candidate over another is always that the one is a better match for the job requirements, even if part of the reason is an adverse reference.*

## Interview the Top Candidates

Before you interview, test. If a test (skills and/or physical) is needed, have all the remaining applicants take it. That sequence is more efficient in terms of time and effort.

The actual interview is the least accurate step of the selection process, if only because most of us don't interview a lot, don't have the necessary skills for it, tend to have biases of which we are unaware, and find the process a bit embarrassing. Have you ever interviewed someone and then realized that you'd spent most of the time talking about your business, the job, and how important it is—and not let the applicant talk? It happens all the time.

Open questions—those that can't be answered with a simple yes or no—elicit the most information. Plan for the interview, ask the questions, and listen to the response. To any response, ask, "Why?"

You want to get the applicant to talk and provide as much "can do" and "will do" information as you need. Prepare: jot down questions before the interview and you will learn more than you would in an unstructured interview. Figure 4-6 offers some suggestions.

- ▶ Are you familiar with _____ (software or computer, for example)?
- ▶ How would you handle a disappointed client or donor?
- ▶ What would you do if _____?
- ▶ What did you like (dislike) about your previous job (your school)?
- ▶ Of all the supervisors (teachers) you've had, describe the one you liked best. Describe the one you liked least.
- ▶ How much pay do you expect for this kind of work?
- ▶ What type of work do you expect to be doing in two years? Five years?
- ▶ If you could pick any job in the world, what would you pick? Why?
- ▶ What's most important to you about a job?
- ▶ If we asked your previous boss about your job performance, what do you think he/she would say?
- ▶ What do you believe are your strong points? Your weak points?

**Figure 4-6.** Sample interview questions

Some questions you may wish to ask may put you on questionable legal ground. Be familiar with the legal guidelines, as shown in Figure 4-7.

| | **You May** | **You May Not** |
| --- | --- | --- |
| Name | Ask for the name (maiden name) of an applicant | Inquire into the national or religious origin of the name, or ask if it was changed |
| Address | Ask for the current address and length of residence. | Ask for a past foreign address. |
| Age, Place of Birth | | Ask the applicant's date of birth, or require birth certificate, naturalization, or baptismal papers. |
| Religion | | Question the applicant's religion, religious beliefs, parish, names of clergy, or religious holidays observed. |
| Race or Color | | Ask questions relating directly to race or color. |

**Figure 4-7.** Screening practices and the law (continued on next page)

|  | **You May** | **You May Not** |
|---|---|---|
| Marital Status | Determine if applicant is married, single, divorced, or widowed. | |
| Number and age of children | Ask the number of dependents, and whether they are in school. | Ask age of children or childcare arrangements. |
| Citizenship | Inquire if applicant is a US citizen. If an alien, you may determine if the applicant has permission to remain in the country and has a work permit. | Inquire whether the applicant's spouse or parents are native born or naturalized, or request dates of naturalization or application papers. |
| Education | Obtain names of schools, level of education, and graduation dates. | Establish a non-job-related educational requirement, or ask the racial, national, or religious affiliation of schools attended. |
| Military Service | Inquire into the applicant's military background, skills learned, and rank attained. | Determine type of discharge, request discharge papers, or inquire into the applicant's foreign military service. |
| Organizations | Inquire into organizations of which the applicant is a member, providing that the organization does not reveal religion, race, color, or national origins of its members. You may ask what offices the applicant held. | Request the names of the organizations. |
| Health Related | Determine height, weight, disability data | Set minimum or maximum height, weight, or other physical requirements that are not directly job related. |

**Figure 4-7.** Screening practices and the law (continued)

Once you have interviewed all of the applicants, make your decision. To prevent the "last interviewed, first hired" syndrome, use Figure 4-8, Selection Summary Sheet, to keep all of the applicants' strong and weak points in mind.

```
┌─────────────────────────────────────────────────────────────────┐
│ Date: _____                                             │
│                                                                   │
│ Interviewer: _____                 │
│                                                                   │
│ Position: _____                       │
│                                                                   │
│ Candidate's Name: _____            │
│                                                                   │
│ Comments: _____   │
│                                                                   │
│ _____       │
│                                                                   │
│ "Can Do" Factors:                                                 │
│                                                                   │
│ _____       │
│                                                                   │
│ _____       │
├───────────────────────────────────────────────────────────────────┤
│ "Will Do" Factors:                                                │
│                                                                   │
│ 1. Stability: _____        │
│                                                                   │
│ 2. Need for job: _____        │
│                                                                   │
│ 3. Attitude toward supervision: _____        │
│                                                                   │
│ 4. Ability to work with others: _____        │
│                                                                   │
│ 5. Skills and experience: _____        │
│                                                                   │
│ 6. Attitudes toward training: _____        │
│                                                                   │
│ 7. Expectations about job: _____        │
│                                                                   │
│ 8. Other factors (specify): _____        │
└─────────────────────────────────────────────────────────────────┘
```

**Figure 4-8.** Selection summary sheet

Use Figure 4-9 only as a jog to your memory. It is not a rating form. If used carefully, it will be legally justifiable. A rating system that applies different weights to different job factors can be a problem: how do you justify, for example, a rating of seven for "expectations about job," rather than eight or six or even nine or five?

Once you make your decision, let the other candidates know that you've hired a candidate you think better matched the requirements of the job. Ask if they would be interested in having their name kept on file for future job openings. If you have followed the steps indicated, most will say, "Please do," and you will build a pool of qualified people interested in joining your organization.

# What About Pay and Fringe Benefits?

You want to pay well enough to attract and retain competent employees, but not more than you have to. At the same time, you want to be sure to be fair: equal pay for equal work makes good business, financial, and legal sense. If your employees think you are unfair or play favorites, you'll be dealing with a severe morale problem.

Compensation consists of two parts: pay (whether salary or wages) and benefits.

## Establish Salary and Wage Levels

Look for current going rates. You can get reasonably up-to-date lists of regional averages, broken down by job, from the Department of Labor's Bureau of Labor Statistics (*www.bls.gov*) or from state employment agencies. You can also get a close approximation by watching newspaper want ads, by asking other nonprofit managers, and sometimes by calling local business schools. If you have established a good relationship with local employment agencies, they'll provide the best salary information of all, since they have to be up-to-date to do their job.

Once you know what the average salaries are for the job (as described in the job description), establish a range going 10 percent lower and higher. You won't be far wrong if you offer the low end to an inexperienced applicant and reserve the higher end for either bargaining or providing room for salary growth that won't put your pay scales out of balance.

For example, if the going rate for a part-time secretary in your area is $15.00 an hour, set your range at $13.50 and $16.50. That allows you to get a competent secretary, have some room for a raise if warranted, and replace him or her if necessary. Someone else may offer a lot more money than you think the job is worth.

## Determine Benefits

What benefits do you offer? Fringe benefits—the other part of the compensation package—amount, on average, to 35 percent of salary. While you will not be able to compete with big companies on some fringe benefits, you can do three things:

- ▶ Make sure that your employees know what benefits they are receiving.
- ▶ Offer them some noncash (and untraditional) benefits that a bigger company cannot.

▶ Most important of all—be able to respond to their needs.

Employee concerns include:

▶ Retirement, financial planning, tax minimization programs

▶ Health care and health insurance

▶ Life and disability (income replacement) insurance

▶ Growth, recognition, achievement, and participation opportunities

▶ Security for their families

▶ Job security

As you put together the compensation package, your concerns include:

▶ Attracting and keeping good employees

▶ Motivating and training personnel

▶ Being fair to all employees

▶ Recognizing employee performance

▶ Protecting employees (insurance, job security)

▶ Providing retirement income

▶ Providing opportunities to build capital

Look at Figure 4-9, List of Possible Fringe Benefits. It may spark some ideas for structuring a benefit plan that helps both you and your employees. Get tax and legal counsel to make sure that you don't create future problems. This is especially important for benefits that apply to you as the owner but not to employees. Also, review retirement programs and insurance.

As you review the list in Figure 4-10, ask the following questions:

▶ Would this be attractive to my employees?

▶ How much will it cost (now and later)?

▶ What are the budget limitations?

▶ Is the plan legal?

▶ Is the plan tax-wise?

▶ What is the purpose of the plan?

▶ Does it fit the needs of my employees?

▶ How extensive should it be?

▶ Who will be covered?

▶ What will the eligibility requirements be?

▶ Should the employees contribute?

**Legally Required:**

(Check with your lawyer and accountant for details, as the particulars change; you want to protect yourself.)

▶ Social Security (FICA)

▶ Workers' compensation insurance

▶ Federal unemployment insurance (FUTA)

▶ Continuation of medical insurance (COBRA) (employers with 20 or more employees)

▶ In some states, state unemployment insurance

▶ In some states, employee disability insurance

▶ Pay while on jury duty or in military reserve

▶ Family and Medical Leave Act

**Direct Cash Benefits:**

(These optional benefits cost you cash.)

▶ Medical expense benefits

▶ Life, accident, and health insurance

▶ Membership in HMOs (health maintenance organizations)

▶ Disability income insurance

▶ Retirement plans

▶ Profit sharing

▶ Dental care, prescription drug, vision care, group life plans

▶ Legal services

**Indirect Cash Benefits:**

(These benefits are costly, valuable, and often overlooked as benefits because they are so common.)

▶ Paid holidays

▶ Paid vacations

▶ Paid sick leave

▶ Paid time off: funeral, "mental health" or personal days, birthdays, dental or medical appointments, attendance at school events

▶ Free lunch, uniform, transportation

▶ Educational benefits

▶ Recreation services (health club membership, for example)

▶ Company trips, parties, celebrations

**Figure 4-9.** List of possible fringe benefits (continued on next page)

**Non-Cash Benefits:**

(These benefits cost, but the costs are hard to calculate.)

- ▶ Flexible time schedules
- ▶ Job sharing
- ▶ Coffee breaks
- ▶ Childcare
- ▶ Release time
- ▶ Sabbaticals, unpaid time off (for long trips, for example)
- ▶ Company teams
- ▶ Personal use of company equipment, facilities
- ▶ Access to company legal and accounting help

**Figure 4-9.** List of possible fringe benefits (continued)

You can probably add to the list. Your imagination is the only barrier. For example, maybe you can let your employees bring their well-behaved dogs to the office.

You have a great deal of flexibility in designing your benefit package— but with this flexibility, there's a lot of red tape. Hence the need for legal and tax counsel. For example, you can establish eligibility requirements of six months' employment before joining a medical insurance plan, but that requirement has to apply to everybody, not just a particular employee. Vendors will explain the ins and outs of eligibility requirements, but it pays to have your attorney make sure that you are indeed legal.

*Many small organizations ask their employees to share some of the costs of insurance programs, especially health and disability insurance.*

Many small organizations ask their employees to share some of the costs of insurance programs, especially health and disability insurance. Membership in a group plan can offer substantial savings to both employer and employee. Limit your premium payments: pay 50 percent of the premium, for example, and have the employee pay the rest. Or pay the entire premium this year, but pass the inevitable premium increases on to the employees, paying the same premium in subsequent years. They get top coverage; you get protected against premium inflation.

## Promote Your Benefits

Make employees aware of the value of the benefits you provide. Fringe benefits are expensive. Once you know what benefits you offer (including the legally mandated benefits), make sure that you communicate that value to your employees.

One way to do this is on the paycheck; unfortunately, that vehicle cannot show some of the less obvious but most valuable benefits that your business can offer. Some insurance companies provide brochures detailing the value of their services to your employees.

We recommend using Figure 4-10, Total Compensation, to keep your employees aware of the extent of their compensation. Fill it out and distribute it once a quarter, when you have quarterly tax statements to provide base information.

Adapt Figure 4-10 to the benefits you offer. Add your contribution to a pension plan or free childcare, if appropriate. The total amount per employee may well give you a jolt the first time you add it all up. It will be more than you expect.

---

Employee Name: _____

During the past quarter, your total compensation included:

Salary/Wages for Quarter:

Social Security paid by company:

Workers' Compensation premium:

Other federal, state, and local premiums:

Health, accident, and life insurance:

Educational benefits:

Total:

Other benefits:

Number of paid vacation days:

Number of paid holidays:

Number of paid personal days:

Other benefits (specify):

Date: _____

---

**Figure 4-10.** Total compensation

# How Do I Get a New Employee up to Speed?

Orientation and training go together. Make orientation the first part of training and you prevent a lot of stress. All of your employees benefit from orientation—working a new person into the group and changing work patterns is not easy. The first day on the job is always confusing, especially for a new employee, although many of the same concerns apply to a newly promoted employee who must learn new ways of dealing with other employees.

*Make orientation the first part of training and you prevent a lot of stress.*

Figure 4-11, First-Day Orientation Form, will help you cover three broad areas when orienting a new employee:

▶ Organizational rules and policies

▶ Introduction to the people who will be working with or supervising the new employee

▶ The physical plant and safety rules

---

Employee Name: _____

Position: _____

Date Hired: _____ Date Started: _____

Person responsible for orientation: _____

Date for review: _____

Employee file opened by: _____ Date: _____

Check box for each item completed.

❏ Application received and filed?

❏ References checked?

❏ Performance test results evaluated and filed?

❏ Date set for evaluation reports?

❏ W4 and insurance forms given to employee?

❏ Employment Eligibility Verification (Form I-9) given to employee?

**Orientation**

**First Day**

Welcome

Show coatroom, coffee machine, bathroom, other amenities

---

**Figure 4-11.** First-day orientation form (continued on next page)

Explain safety regulations

Review: working hours, lunch hours, coffee breaks, parking

Review job description

Describe work

Introduce to coworkers

Introduce to supervisor

Show operation

Observe employee perform

Let employee know when you are available

Check progress at the end of first day; ask questions

**Figure 4-11.** First-day orientation form (continued)

Set a time for a review with the employee at the end of his/her first week on the job. You want to answer his or her questions, improve the orientation process, and make sure the new employee is settling in well.

Review the job description with the employee and make sure he or she knows the responsibilities. As you review the job description, set performance goals with the employee. When it's time to review and evaluate his or her performance, you'll have a good agenda to work from.

*One week should give a clue to the employee's training needs, especially if you ask the employee what kind of skills he or she needs to acquire to do the job.*

A new employee should receive an orientation review at the end of the first week. Adjusting to the new work environment and fitting into a different group of co-workers is difficult and confusing, so you want to make the transition as smooth as possible. When you review the first week, let the employee ask questions. You may have to do some prompting, since he or she won't necessarily know what to ask.

The brief interview at the end of the first week is important. Try to get the employee to talk as much as possible—the first week establishes lasting impressions for both of you.

## Training

Once the employee has had a chance to acclimate to your organization, training to sharpen his or her skills may be indicated. One week should give a clue to the employee's needs, especially if you ask the employee what kind of skills he or she needs to acquire to do the job.

Employee Name: _____

Position: _____

Reviewed by: _____

Date: _____

Date for next review: _____

Check off each item after discussing it with employee:

❏ Review progress

❏ Discuss training needs

❏ Set performance goals with employee

❏ Write down performance goals; give copy to employee

❏ Review pay procedures

❏ Review benefits (see Figure 4-11)

❏ Set date for next review

Comments: _____

_____

**Figure 4-12.** First-week orientation form

Training provides a lot for an employee: a sense of growth and achievement, knowledge that management (you) is interested in improving his or her skills, and recognition of his or her potential to advance. By making training available early, you also make a statement: you show from the start that you want your employees to grow.

You have to look ahead to the needs of your NPO—so don't confine training to new hires or to problem employees. One of the biggest selling points for a small organization is a reputation for helping employees to grow into more responsible positions. This opportunity and encouragement significantly reduces turnover and personnel costs; employees tend to stay where they feel like they can grow. Few people like to stick with a dead-end job; those who do aren't the kind of employees you want anyway.

To promote from within, you need employees who are well qualified. That calls for serious training efforts.

What kinds of training are appropriate? It depends on your employees, their skills and interests, your plans, and the future needs of your organiza-

*You have to look ahead to the needs of your NPO—so don't confine training to new hires or to problem employees.*

77

tion. As with other aspects of management, a little planning goes a long way. Comparing job descriptions with the people available is one part of the planning process. Another is to ask these three questions:

1. What skills will these jobs demand in the future?
2. What skills are getting rusty, outmoded, obsolete—and how can they be replaced, sharpened, upgraded?
3. How about interpersonal skills, sales training, pre-retirement training, and other less tangible training needs?

*Most training efforts concentrate on job-related skills, but other training pays big morale dividends.*

Most training efforts concentrate on job-related skills, but other training pays big morale dividends. Even if the skill an employee wants to pick up seems useless, think of it this way: an employee willing to put time and effort into learning new skills is apt to be more valuable over the long run than an employee content with his or her present skills.

On-the-job training (OJT) is the most common method. Decide what to teach, who is to teach it, and what results you are looking for. If you do the training, you benefit by getting to know the employee better, gaining a clearer understanding of the process or skill being taught, and perhaps finding ways to improve the operation.

In OJT the employee is shown, step by step, how a process is performed. Then the employee performs the operation, under close supervision, until he or she does it right. Finally, evaluate the performance, offer suggestions for improvement if needed, and jointly set some goals for a review at a later date.

This can take enormous amounts of your time—and your time is valuable. On the other hand, it can be done over time, in odd moments, and is the easiest mode of training to master.

Apprentice programs link the new employee to a skilled employee, who teaches the skills and tricks of the trade. For example, a fundraising telemarketer may start out on the front line with the employees who provide your services, to become familiar with those services and the people who benefit from them, and then help deliver services, before finally making calls. This step-by-step process works if you can afford the time.

Job rotation lets employees try out other jobs in the organization. This makes your employees more flexible, is excellent for morale because employees don't get tracked into one slot, and makes it easier to replace key employees.

The drawback is lower productivity—but the pluses of well-rounded employees who understand many jobs may be worth the cost. You can intro-

| Training Method | Pros | Cons |
| --- | --- | --- |
| 1. On the Job | Low cost, direct benefit to company, can be controlled | Ties up other productive workers, machinery; need skilled teacher |
| 2. Conference or Coaching | Can be tailored to individual, low cost, flexible | Ties up supervisor, can lead to unrealistic hopes if not carefully monitored |
| 3. Apprentice | Highly focused, easy to measure progress, some government programs available | High cost of paying apprentice; time taken away from skilled workers |
| 4. Classroom | Allows many people to be taught at once, cost-effective for groups | Limited interaction, cost of released time and teacher may be excessive; retention lower than hands on |
| 5. Programmed instruction | Low cost, portable, very good for some technical material | Hard to find for specific skills; too costly to develop in-house |
| 6. Rotational: Let employees trade jobs | Good for morale, tests employees in various capacities | Apt to slow down productivity, requires a large number of people and jobs for effective use; may raise hopes too far |
| 7. Projects and committees | Low cost, wide exposure to management, broad range of possible tasks | Time consuming; can be dominated by wrong people; hard on timid |
| 8. In-house training | Accurately pinpoint needs and skills; easy to measure and control | High cost tends to inflate fixed training costs, unless closely managed; may need professional help. |
| 9. Professional clubs, trade and business associations | Exposure to new ideas and new techniques; wide range of programs; good for trade relations | May lead to heavy recruitment of your best people; uneven quality of programs; cost may exceed benefits |
| 10. Role playing or management games | Can help air views, feelings, alleviate internal problems; can help you understand your own management style. | Can degenerate into expensive game; low carryover into work situation. |

**Figure 4-13.** Training alternatives

duce job rotation in a limited way, a few hours a week. Your employees will look at job rotation as a fringe benefit.

The other forms of training in Figure 4-14 all have their place, though they are less common in smaller organizations. Still, with the competition for skilled and willing workers on the rise in most areas, consider using these other forms of training. People like to learn. Give your employees the opportunity and encouragement, and all of you will benefit.

---

Employee Name: _____

Reviewed with employee:     Yes _____     No _____

Date: _____

By: _____

Improvement suggested in these areas:

Suggested solutions: _____

Training scheduled to start: _____

❏ Copy to employee

❏ Original to file

---

**Figure 4-14.** Employee training needs

# Appendix: Examples of Job Descriptions

## For an executive director:

The Executive Director is an employee of the Women's Business Center, with the following responsibilities:

1. Hire, train, and manage staff. The Executive Committee will work with the Executive Director to devise a staffing plan.

2. Maintain membership records for the WBC. This will include database maintenance, handling dues collection, renewal notices, mailing labels, membership, statistics, etc.

3. Act as fiscal agent for the WBC, maintaining bank accounts, accounts payable and receivable, handling cash when appropriate, bookkeeping, and maintaining financial records.

4. Report to the Board of Directors of the Women's Business Center—specifically to the Executive Committee. The Executive Director will provide financial reports to the Board on a regular basis and as requested. These will include an annual end-of-year financial report. The Executive Director will work with the Board (and specifically with the Secretary-Treasurer and the Budget Committee) to establish an annual budget for the WBC.

5. Provide administrative support to WBC and Board activities. This may include print and distribution of membership materials, such as ballots, publications, division and interest group materials.

6. Provide support for annual conferences of the WBC. Conference support may include exhibitor communications and coordination, and work with the Conference Planning Committee.

7. In addition to the above, specific tasks that are part of the Executive Director's duties are:
   - accounting for Association funds;
   - having accounts audited annually and providing audit reports to the Board;
   - maintaining appropriate postal permits;
   - producing mailing labels;
   - handling member expense reimbursements;
   - maintaining and filing records for tax and other business purposes;
   - maintaining the WBC's membership in selected organizations;
   - attending WBC Board meetings;
   - updating and maintaining the Manual of Procedures, Bylaws, etc. and distributing them to all incoming officers of the WBC.

8. Other administrative duties as assigned by the Board of Directors.

**Qualifications:**

**Required:**

- ▶ knowledge of and/or experience with professional associations and/or other nonprofit organizations;
- ▶ organizational skills, including demonstrated attention to detail;
- ▶ ability to understand and analyze financial data;
- ▶ ability to take initiative and be a self-starter;
- ▶ ability to efficiently schedule time and activities;
- ▶ ability to maintain effectiveness in varying environments and with varying tasks, responsibilities, or people;
- ▶ excellent oral and written communication skills;
- ▶ demonstrated computer skills;
- ▶ flexibility to travel to meetings as required by Board of Directors;
- ▶ bondable.

**Desired:**

- ▶ bookkeeping and managerial accounting experience;
- ▶ knowledge of business education and development programs.

The Board of Directors (or its Executive Committee) shall annually evaluate the Executive Director's performance of his/her duties.

**Salary range:** $3,500 to $4,500/month.

**Hours:** Full-time (40 hours/week). Some evening and weekend work will be required. Intermittent travel (average four days/month) for conferences and meetings.

**Job Specifications:**

1. Proven communication skills. This person must be able to:
   - ▶ write clearly and simply
   - ▶ communicate clearly with professional clientele
   - ▶ give speeches to communicate the work of the WBC to the community

2. Business development experience, preferably with small businesses:
   - ▶ work with Small Business Administration and similar programs
   - ▶ work with bankers, business leaders, and community leaders
   - ▶ collaborate with other agencies

3. Aptitudes:
   - ▶ ability to master financial and business terminology
   - ▶ work to deadlines with minimal supervision

4. Education and experience should demonstrate required skills and aptitudes.

We reserve the right to change or revise duties and responsibilities as the need arises. This document is not a written or implied contract of employment.

## For a program committee volunteer:

**Job title:** member program committee

**Job objective:** Oversight of program effectiveness; help staff develop appropriate programs; enhance the value of WBC programs for the membership; assist staff in promoting programs

**List of duties:** attend and actively participate in program committee meetings; prepare for meetings in advance with such research or other actions as may be needed; follow through on commitments to the program committee in a timely manner

**Expectations:** exercise best judgment about present and future programs with the overall mission of the WBC in mind

**Time commitment:** one meeting a month, usually for one hour; extra time commitment depends on the specific actions suggested in the monthly meetings but will not normally exceed two hours per month.

**Roles and relationships:** Chair reports to Board of Directors via Executive Committee monthly; delivers report summary to the Board of Directors meetings.

**Notification of absence:** Call Jane Torrey!

## For an executive committee member:

**Job Title:** member executive committee

**Job objective:** review and distill monthly committee reports submitted by committee chairs; assist Executive Director in his/her role by providing advice and counsel; set quarterly Board of Directors meeting agenda;

**List of duties:** attend and actively participate in executive committee meetings; prepare for meetings in advance with such research or other actions as may be needed; follow through on commitments to the executive committee in a timely manner

**Expectations:** exercise best judgment about present and future programs with the overall mission of the WBC in mind

**Time commitment:** one meeting a month, usually for no more than two hours; extra time commitment depends on the specific actions suggested in the monthly meetings but will not normally exceed two hours per month.

**Roles and relationships:** the Executive committee acts as the steering committee for the BoD, assigns priorities (as in setting the agenda) for membership and board decisions, keeps track of bylaws and finances....

**Notification of absence:** Call Lisa or Connie!

HELP
HERE

# Chapter 5

# Managing People, Part 3

IF YOU FOLLOW THE ADVICE AND GUIDELINES IN CHAPTERS 3 AND 4, THIS chapter should not be as important. However, it's still necessary.

## How Can I Keep Good Employees?

First, you have to hire well. Determine the job need, write a job description, recruit well, and select carefully from a number of qualified applicants. And you need to orient new employees to help them fit and feel comfortable from the start. You also need to train new and newly promoted employees. Pay them adequately.

Second, treat your employees well. The basic rule of personnel management is simple: do unto others as you would have others do unto you. Keep in mind what you would want in a job:

- ▶ Fair wages
- ▶ Job security
- ▶ Agreeable working conditions: reasonable hours, safe, clean and well-lit workspace, a pleasant environment
- ▶ A sense of improving your talents, worth, and status

▶ A sense of contribution to the company and the community

▶ Respect for and from management

These are *satisfiers*, to borrow the term used by Frederick Herzberg, a psychologist who studied motivation in the workplace. All are required to prevent employee dissatisfaction.

Third, recognize that you don't motivate employees. Employees motivate themselves. All you can do is destroy their motivation—unless you make it a careful policy to provide more than the satisfiers listed above. Your employees are adults. Treat them accordingly. The more autonomy you encourage, the more control they have over their work and the better they will perform for you.

There are exceptions. That's why personnel management is necessary. You set rules and standards and you help employees set objectives that contribute to the achievement of your mission. Performance evaluations serve a number of needs, not the least of which is to fairly reward those who are making progress and provide guidance for those who are not.

This doesn't mean that you become a patsy for lazy or careless workers. Even in a nonprofit you have to make a profit to stay in business and meet your budget and pursue your mission. Keeping unproductive employees on staff is a quick way to destroy everyone's job and jeopardize the organization. You lose the respect of good employees by setting double standards for unproductive employees—a violation of the fairness principle. If an employee is not willing or not able to do the job, you have to take steps. Sometimes discipline or termination is needed. Part of the job of keeping good employees involves weeding out bad ones.

*If an employee is not willing or not able to do the job, you have to take steps.*

Fourth, to keep good employees, you must understand that all employees have needs for:

▶ Growth

▶ Recognition

▶ Achievement

▶ Participation

To meet these needs, you have to provide plenty of:

▶ Effort

Remember that employees motivate themselves. Your job is to provide opportunities for them to exercise their skills and efforts.

85

1. **Growth.** Employees grow through training, stretching skills and talents, taking on more responsibility. Some growth opportunities come from outside the organization—through, for example, participating in amateur theater, learning to play a new sport or instrument, or becoming a parent. Encourage your employees to grow, both at work and in their personal lives.

2. **Recognition.** One reason for periodic performance reviews is to make sure that you recognize your employees' contributions. Nobody likes to toil without being recognized—if their work is worth their hire, they want it to be noticed. If they need to improve, fine. That's a form of recognition; it shows they aren't being overlooked. It's easy to forget the importance of this recognition factor. "Management by walking around" is effective because it provides managers chances to recognize employees' contributions and achievements. A small NPO is a perfect environment for this kind of management.

3. **Achievement.** A sense of achievement comes from doing something difficult—reaching a goal, helping the organization attain a tough objective, mastering a new skill or machine, solving a problem. A well-managed organization provides opportunities for achievement and growth, which can then be recognized (sincerely) and perhaps rewarded. Note the "sincerely": long term, all recognition has to be based on achievement or else it degenerates into flattery, which will get you nowhere.

*A sense of achievement comes from doing something difficult—reaching a goal, helping the organization attain a tough objective, mastering a new skill or machine, solving a problem.*

4. **Participation.** Remember the team analogy. One advantage a small operation has over a big one is that managers are closer to employees. You can involve them in their work life and keep them constantly aware of how well the organization is doing. What are the goals? Are we making progress? How can I contribute?

   A lot of management practice centers on establishing a sense of participation. Look at management by objectives, in which you and the employee set objectives together, establish dates to reach goals en route to achieving the objectives, and a come to an agreement on how to measure progress along the way.

   Sophisticated? Yes. Easy to do? Yes—if you take the time to provide the opportunity for your employees to participate in establishing and monitoring their own work. Who benefits? All of you.

5. **Effort.** It takes a lot of effort—consistent, attentive-to-detail effort from you and your employees. There is no substitute. As the owner, you have to provide the ongoing energy and direction that an organization runs on. And that takes effort.

There are plenty of tools available to help your employees maintain their motivation. Any standard management textbook is full of them—but it comes down to treating your employees the way you would want to be treated yourself. Everyone wants honest appreciation and recognition of their efforts and contributions, respect as an individual, opportunities for growth, and recognition.

You and your employees are in this together—not as enemies but as partners. They may need leading, organizing, and coordinating (that's your job), but they will perform as well as they can if you don't get in their way.

This means you need to plan and communicate. Not easy or simple, but well within your reach.

Bill Scott called on his 30-plus years of management experience in the Thomson School of Applied Science at the University of New Hampshire to provide the list of questions in Figure 5.1 to help managers understand the elements of his GRAPE (growth, recognition, achievement, participation, effort) theory of management.

*Everyone wants honest appreciation and recognition of their efforts and contributions, respect as an individual, opportunities for growth, and recognition.*

### 1. Growth

▸ Do you promote from within whenever possible?

▸ Do you give good recommendations and help employees who leave for better jobs?

▸ Do you train and encourage employees to learn about everything they can?

▸ Do you institute and encourage workshops?

▸ Do you pay partial tuition for schooling related to your company?

▸ Do you counsel and initiate conversations to show employees how to improve or grow or develop a career?

▸ Do you encourage membership in professional clubs or organizations?

▸ Do you publicize promotions?

▸ Do you explain to employees why someone has been brought in from outside? Show them how they can become as well qualified?

▸ Do you rotate jobs among employees?

▸ Do you use flexible work hours?

▸ Do you have a suggestion program?

▸ Do you use meaningful performance evaluations?

### 2. Recognition

▸ Do you know when an employee does an exceptionally good job—and let him or her know you know?

▸ Do you know your employees' hobbies, interests, needs, and goals?

**Figure 5-1.** GRAPE checklist (continued on next page)

> ▶ Do you provide time to listen to individual employees?
> ▶ Do you meet with each employee for performance evaluations?
> ▶ Do you ask employees to help improve business operations?
> ▶ Do you help employees improve their skills?
>
> **3. Achievement**
> ▶ Do you allow your employees chances to excel? To do the job their way?
> ▶ Do you explain what you want accomplished and allow your employees to figure out how to achieve those goals?
> ▶ Do you set assignments that stretch employees' abilities?
> ▶ Do you think your employees are capable of doing more or better work?
> ▶ Do you provide the tools, time, and other resources to improve their performance?
> ▶ Do you applaud their off-work achievements?
> ▶ Do you allow employees to use their heads in achieving your goals?
>
> **4. Participation**
> ▶ Do you ask your employees' advice? Solicit their opinions?
> ▶ Do you implement their suggestions?
> ▶ Do you encourage employees to speak up?
> ▶ Do you practice listening?
> ▶ Can employees shape their work environment to some degree: hours, work groups, plants, pictures, and so on?
> ▶ Do you use management by objectives?

**Figure 5-1.** GRAPE checklist (continued)

Review these questions quarterly. If you can answer most of them "Yes," you are providing a working environment that allows employees to contribute more than 100-percent effort.

# Evaluations and Salary Reviews

Performance evaluations are important for three reasons. First, they assess your employees' progress toward fulfilling the requirements of their jobs. Second, they provide your employees with benchmarks and give them a way to measure their own growth and achievement. Third, they'll ultimately help you improve your own management skills.

There are six basic steps in performance evaluations.

1. Prepare performance objectives with the employee, based on the job description, your knowledge of the employee, and your understanding of

the special circumstances (if any) your NPO is operating under, such as competition and general economic circumstances. Do this alone, before meeting with your employee, so you have a framework.

2. Discuss the objectives with the employee. Explain how they help the company reach its goals. Adjust them so both of you feel they are attainable, worth achieving, and measurable in the time frame involved.

3. Watch the employee's performance during the time until the next evaluation (six months at most). If corrections are in order, suggest them. Provide training. If praise is in order, give it. Keep notes—with dates and details—to substantiate the evaluation.

4. Evaluate the employee's performance against the objectives, before the evaluation interview.

5. Discuss your evaluation with the employee. Be prepared to justify your evaluation with specifics; the notes you've taken (Step 3) will show the employee that you recognize his or her accomplishments, strengths, and shortcomings.

*For any rating with room for improvement—and all have room because nobody is perfect—ask the employee how he or she could improve.*

For any rating with room for improvement—and all have room because nobody is perfect—ask the employee how he or she could improve. Since most employees know what they could do better in certain parts of their job, this won't be threatening. Your aim is to improve performance so your organization can achieve its goals.

6. Take whatever action is appropriate. If the employee deserves praise, provide it. If the employee just doesn't fit in with your organization, consider firing him or her. Most of the time, though, the appropriate action will consist of setting new objectives with the employee for the next evaluation period, suggesting training or other opportunities for improving performance, and helping the employee get ready for more responsible or challenging work.

Sometimes an employee will be defensive. That's one reason to be prepared with as many factual, dated observations as possible. There is no substitute for a comment such as "You had an argument with a customer June 3 and another one August 5. Do you think you can change that type of response even when the customer is wrong?"

Note that the performance review does not include discussing salary. The last step—taking appropriate action—may include granting a raise or withholding one. But it may not. Ideally, the salary review is a separate issue, based on performance but also including other factors, such as the employee's seniority, his or her contribution to organizational goals, and even his or her needs.

While a small NPO cannot build in automatic pay raises, almost all do give them. Employees expect raises—and employers seem to expect to give them.

# Salary Reviews

When you established salary ranges extending ten percent lower and higher than the average salary, you tacitly set a limit on what a job is worth to your organization. Keep these averages and ranges current. They change, sometimes dramatically, and you don't want to be caught in a rigid position with outdated numbers.

Here are some factors that you may want to consider in deciding on salary increases:

- ▶ Organizational cash flow and budgets. Salaries are fixed costs.
- ▶ Seniority has a place—long-term loyal employees contribute in more than the obvious ways.
- ▶ Two small salary increases per year have a more positive effect than one bigger increase and hurt your cash flow less. A raise of $10 a week in January and another $10 in June add up to $780 for the year. A raise of $20 a week in March also adds $780 to the outflow, but the employee will usually feel that a year between pay raises is a long time. (And a $20 raise in January amounts to $1,040 per year.)
- ▶ If you keep your employees aware of the financial condition of your organization, they may be less demanding when times are tight. Most people prefer a secure job and, as long as the wages are fair, will postpone a raise.
- ▶ There are noncash raises you might offer instead of or with cash raises: time off, extra holidays, help with tuition, a change in job structure, more flexible hours.
- ▶ People are as sensitive about salaries as about any topic that affects their lives. Make sure that salary information is private—but also make sure that salaries reflect contributions to the organization. An unfair salary range, where two people are paid very differently for no apparent reason, is a major source of employee anger; it can also present legal problems. Keep the fairness principle in mind.
- ▶ A salary review is a compensation review. During a salary review, point out the value of the fringe benefits and keep the employee aware of increases in these benefits. Use Figure 4-11, Total Compensation, to drive home the value of the fringe benefits.

# Promotions

The performance review is a good time to discuss promotion possibilities. While small NPOs do not have a lot of promotion possibilities—a three-employee NPO with an executive director and two employees has little room for a promotion—you can provide new challenges. A job can be expanded: more responsibility, higher goals, more employee control.

If you can provide a promotion and the employee is qualified and willing to accept the promotion, great! There are few morale boosters as strong as the chance to be promoted on the basis of actual performance and contribution to the business. Once more: promotions based on other grounds will be perceived as unfair and cause endless problems. Be fair.

Treat a promotion the same way you treat a hire: make sure the best person gets the position. Then, treat the employee you promote as a new hire: go through the parts of the orientation procedure that make the most sense. (Use your judgment.) Changing work and peer relationships can be very difficult, so the newly promoted employee will need support.

*Treat a promotion the same way you treat a hire: make sure the best person gets the position.*

Make sure you have an up-to-date job description for both the new positions the employee will have and for the position the employee is leaving. Then fill the vacated job—from within if possible: another promotion possibility. A qualified employee has a huge advantage over an outsider: familiarity with the business. You know how the employee works and deals with responsibility and you can train him or her to fit the new job description.

Promoting an employee alters work patterns, leaving some duties uncovered. Be careful.

A promotion can also affect morale. If other employees think they should have received the promotion, or at least been considered for it, make sure they understand that you chose the person best matched to the requirements of the job. If you always promote fairly, no problem. If the promotion is based on other grounds, you may find yourself open to legal action.

Follow up on the newly promoted employee—at the end of the first week, after a few weeks on the job, and after a month. Make it clear that you're available if he or she wants to talk; this is particularly important if the employee is now managing other employees. Look for training needs—and provide whatever training is needed.

Salary increases and promotions go together. Fortunately, you can tie the increase to performance, setting objectives and timing to achieve those objectives with the newly promoted employee. Remember: a small raise now and another small one in six months are more appreciated than larger raises given less frequently.

When you and the newly promoted employee set objectives together, be prepared for some unrealistic expectations. Don't be surprised, for example, to have the employee set goals that cannot be reached. Enthusiasm is great, so be as gentle as possible in using your experience and understanding of the organization to adjust the goals. Again, provide facts. If the employee wants to spend $75,000 to gain a $50,000 grant increase, let him or her down gently.

*Performance evaluations and promotions are among the best morale-boosting and motivation-sustaining tools you have.*

Performance evaluations and promotions are among the best morale-boosting and motivation-sustaining tools you have. So, keep the evaluations constant, objective, factual, and fair. Your objective is not to find fault and hoard up notes so you can blast employees—it's to identify strengths and weaknesses, correct or applaud as soon as possible, maintain a fair, factual basis for promotions and salary increases, and help your organization attain its objectives.

When you set objectives and performance evaluation criteria with the employee, you achieve a number of important management goals. GRAPE and its accompanying management-by-objectives style works. It provides the benchmarks needed to chart improvement, helps employees stretch their abilities, provides another channel of communication, and helps maintain the sense of fairness and equity that everyone wants.

# Management by Objectives

Management by objectives (MBO) is an augmented approach to performance evaluation in which the employee participates in setting goals and objectives and provides input into the means to attain those goals. Figure 5-2, Preliminary Goal Setting, will help you use this powerful approach.

MBO proceeds in six steps.

1. Update the job description with the employee's help. Do this together and you gain the employee's cooperation. You might want to start with

## Some MBO Requirements

MBO requires that you:

▶ Know what you want the employee to accomplish,
▶ Inform the employee of your expectations,
▶ Observe and evaluate the employee's performance,
▶ Discuss that evaluation with the employee, and
▶ Take action.

a very sketchy job description and then fill it in with the employee's help. The review and insights provided by your employee are valuable in themselves; he or she is closer to the action and in some ways knows the job as well as you do.

2. Draft a statement of the objective. Figure 5-2 helps; have the employee fill one out too. When you sit down together to set the objectives for the quarter or six months, you will both be prepared. This doesn't mean that you let the employee take over your management prerogatives. Far from it—you have to revise and focus the objectives to fit in with other company goals. But you are saying, loud and clear, that you expect the

---

**I. Performance Objectives: Employee Preliminary Goals**

Employee: _____    Date proposed: _____

For period _____ to _____    To be reviewed: _____

Basic job description (attach copy if available):

**II. Objectives I can reasonably accomplish**

  **Example:** 100% accuracy is not realistic, but improving from 90 to 95% may be.

  _____

  _____

  _____

**III. Measures of success**

  **Example:** Dollar amount, hours, percentage of measurable quantities, averages.

  _____

  _____

  _____

**IV. In order to accomplish these objectives, I need:**

  **Example:** additional tools, training, personnel, time, money.

  _____

  _____

  _____

---

**Figure 5-2.** Preliminary goal setting

employee to think, be creative, become involved, and take charge of his or her job.

3. Review the employee's draft with the employee. "Open covenants openly arrived at," one of the 14 points proposed by President Woodrow Wilson in 1918, was a good political ideal to move peace negotiations beyond the traditional method of secret diplomacy practiced in Europe. It's an ideal for employer/employee relationships, too.

   Encourage the employee by taking his or her ideas seriously. There are three possibilities here:

   ▶ The employee sets goals that are too high.

   ▶ The employee sets goals that are too low.

   ▶ The employee sets goals that agree with yours.

   Employees tend to initially set goals that are unrealistically high. Such goals are frustrating. Negotiate them downward.

   In the second case, be firm. You usually know which employees will set low goals. To raise them, focus on the goals, not the person.

   Sometimes you'll have to dictate the goals—but rarely. More often, if you ask how the employee set the goals, explain why you think they could be higher, and perhaps compare them with other goals or statistics, you can gain agreement. Sometimes employees are down on themselves and need encouragement: "I bet you could gain that 12 percent.... How can I help you?"

   If the employee's goals coincide with yours, rejoice. Find out how the employee decided on those goals, try to improve them marginally, and compare your goal-setting methods with the employee's.

4. Have the employee draft a performance appraisal. Since you and the employee both know what was expected, this is a bookkeeping task. What is of most interest to you is the comment section: why did the employee meet or fail to meet the objectives? Figure 5-3 provides a framework for this.

   The objectives come straight from Figure 5-2, the results are based on performance, and the comments provide the kind of information you want to improve performance in the future. Save these forms; they are a source of ideas for future business improvements.

5. Discuss the results with the employee. Keep your ears open and your mouth shut; you want to learn, which means you have to listen to the employee. Ask questions, but don't provide the answers. Try to find out

Employee Name: _____ Date: _____

Objective: _____

Results: _____

_____

Comments: _____

_____

_____

**Figure 5-3.** Performance appraisal

how and why the employee attained objectives or not. Maybe the causes are external to the organization: competition, economics, legal changes. Maybe the causes are beyond the employee's control: changes in organizational strategies, inadequate fundraising, lack of advertising and marketing efforts. The aim is not to be punitive, but to enable the employee to attain those objectives in the future.

Note the importance of communication throughout this process. When you review the employee's performance appraisal with the employee, try to find out about any needs—for training, equipment, resources, or whatever. Sometimes employees are hesitant about asking for help.

6. Start over again. Get out the job description and update it.

MBO may not be the best method for everyone, but in small companies it is particularly powerful. It helps employees make contributions to the company beyond the average, boosts morale, and sets up a feedback system for checking progress.

*MBO helps employees make contributions to the company beyond the average, boosts morale, and sets up a feedback system for checking progress.*

# Problem Employees

How you deal with a problem employee depends. It depends on the employee. It depends on the cause of the problem. It depends on the problem itself. It depends on the amount of factual information (dated, objective information—written down and saved) you have about the employee's behavior. It depends on what procedures you have established (either deliberately or through habitual practice) to deal with problem employees.

The legal ramifications can be severe. So can the economic consequences. Federal unemployment (FUTA) taxes and state unemployment taxes may skyrocket. You may need legal help at $250/hour. You may find that a former employee is badmouthing your organization and causing problems that will have a price tag later.

Dealing with problem employees really means dealing with problem behaviors. Unless you are a professionally trained counselor, your job is not concerned with the employee but with the problems the employee's behavior is causing your organization.

## Assess the Problem

*You can correct inefficiencies through training, job reorganization, rescheduling, or transferring the employee to a job better matched to his or her capabilities.*

Before taking any action, try to determine what kind of problem you are dealing with. Employee problems fall into two broad categories: inefficiencies and misconduct.

You can correct inefficiencies through training, job reorganization, rescheduling, or transferring the employee to a job better matched to his or her capabilities. Misconduct problems are less tractable.

## Dealing with Inefficiency

Procedures for handling inefficiencies are clear. The preceding section set up review procedures and suggested methods of handling problems due to inefficiencies.

If the inefficiency is due to outside pressure or to the job, try to identify the cause of the problem. Sometimes it will solve itself; sometimes just sharing a problem with another person provides needed relief.

Inefficiency often stems from a mismatch between the employee and the job, usually a lack of skills or training. In these cases, review the job standards, point out the unsatisfactory performance, and see if additional time or training solves the problem. If it doesn't, transfer the employee or change the job. You want to show good faith in case the employee has to be fired, which is a last resort.

## Dealing with Misconduct

Employee misconduct problems are harder to handle. Sometimes misconduct is due to outside pressures—maybe a marital or family problem, or a difficult neighbor, or a poor investment that causes a lot of concern. The misconduct may be due to a job-related problem: a personality conflict, trouble with a customer, pressure from other workers, boredom with the current job, inability to handle the pressure. It may also be caused by substance abuse or other psychological or emotional problems.

If you approach an employee who is exhibiting bizarre or destructive behavior—habitual tardiness or absenteeism, rudeness to customers, inability to concentrate—and focus on the behavior rather than the person, most of the time the employee will respond positively.

If the behavior poses a danger to anyone, put safety first and don't hesitate to call in professional help. Otherwise, follow a written, well-communicated disciplinary procedure. See Figures 5-4 and 5-5 for some guidelines.

Fill in the blanks as appropriate.

But if you suspect the problem to be substance abuse, proceed with caution. Substance abusers will often deny that their problem is alcohol or some other drug-related problem and are extraordinarily good at laying the blame on other people. Get professional help. Employee Assistance Plans (EAPs) are becoming more common and more affordable. If none is available in your area, call the local Alcoholics Anonymous and ask what they recommend; they will know what assistance is available.

Figure 5-4, Disciplinary Guidelines, is not totally rigid. It's a guide that you can post or give to all employees. People like to know what the limits are; if you have to proceed to the more drastic steps (suspension, firing), an outline such as this helps everyone understand the rules.

If the problem is misconduct—intentional and willful or "repeatedly negligent" behavior—communicate the work rules, advise and carefully define the violations in question, and attempt to change the behavior with progressively more intense discipline. (See Figure 5-5.)

If this doesn't work, provide whatever review procedure you have established before firing the employee. Once again, you have to be fair, make a good faith attempt to salvage the situation—and then you can get rid of the problem employee. Your review procedure may be as simple as meeting with the employee offsite—but it must be the same for all employees.

## Document!

Whatever the problem and whatever the causes, make sure to thoroughly and completely document your side of the story. Unfortunately, as the employer you have to lean over backwards to protect your organization (and even your personal assets) against legal actions that make little or no sense. Knowing that, protect yourself. The procedures you should follow are designed to show that you have made a good-faith attempt to treat all of your employees equally and consistently.

| Incident | First Offense | Second Offense | Third Offense | Fourth Offense |
|---|---|---|---|---|
| 1. Absent, no call | | | | |
| 2. Walking off job, no reason or notice given | | | | |
| 3. Arguing with employees | | | | |
| 4. Arguing with clients | | | | |
| 5. Fighting with clients or with employees | | | | |
| 6. Intimidation, harassment (sexual or other) of employees | | | | |
| 7. Insubordination | | | | |
| 8. Purposeful destruction of organization property | | | | |
| 9. Theft | | | | |
| 10. Possession or sale of illegal drugs or alcohol on organization property | | | | |
| 11. Intoxication or under the influence of illegal drugs on organization property | | | | |
| 12. Ignoring safety rules | | | | |

Key: O = oral reminder    W = written reminder    SP = suspended with pay
     SW = suspended without pay    F = fire

**Figure 5-4.** Disciplinary guidelines

For minor problems, such as chronic tardiness or excessive absenteeism, the cure is to make sure that the employee knows his or her contribution to the company is important. Usually all that you have to do is give an oral reminder and pay attention to his or her response; if the problem persists, then begin the steps outlined above.

Provide a clear disciplinary process and follow it. Make no exceptions that you cannot justify. Chronic troublemakers don't stick around where procedures are clear and consistent—and they can't cause problems for you later if you maintain clear records of dates, names, and facts to support your side of the argument.

If a problem arises that you think will lead to progressively more serious disciplinary actions, follow the checklist in Figure 5-5. Keep notes—with dates—to substantiate the content of discussions and counseling efforts.

For minor incidents, use oral reminders immediately. Don't store grievances. Solve the problem instead. Collect and evaluate facts—not feelings or assumptions—and make notes covering dates and results.

---

Employee Name: _____

Describe behavior(s): _____

_____

For each of the following, record, date, and initial:        Initial and Date

Oral reminders                                                _____

Suspension with pay                                           _____

Final written notice                                          _____

Termination:

Final paycheck                                                _____

Other personnel documents (specify)

_____                               _____

_____                               _____

_____                               _____

Exit interview                                                _____

Explanation of appeal procedure                              _____

Explanation of severance pay                                 _____

Explanation of insurance procedures                          _____

Return of organization property (specify)

_____                               _____

_____                               _____

_____                               _____

---

**Figure 5-5.** Checklist for employee problems

If the problem persists for a single moderate incident or if the employee fails to respond to several oral reminders, take the next step. State the violation clearly, in writing, with dates, names, facts (no hearsay, anger, or phrases that could be interpreted as insults). Review this report with the offending employee, get him or her to sign it, give him or her a copy, and keep the original for your files.

The next step is either a suspension or a final written notice. Reserve this for either a single incident of severe misconduct or for a final warning to improve.

Advise the employee that his or her job and income are in immediate danger.

If the facts are in doubt, suspend the employee with pay. Then investigate thoroughly.

The last resort is a final written notice. Give the employee a copy. Keep the original for your files.

If it is necessary to fire the employee, here is the procedure:

▶ Make sure you have a valid reason, based on facts and documented to ensure that the procedure has been fair. If there is *any* doubt, ask your lawyer's advice.

▶ Prepare the paperwork: last paycheck and other personnel documents (such as insurance notification). Be sure your records illustrate the steps taken as outlined above.

▶ Prepare for the exit interview. (See Figure 5-6.) Select the time and a place that ensures privacy.

▶ Notify the employee. Employees who have gone through the steps of the disciplinary process usually are expecting to be fired, but be prepared for either anger or tears.

▶ Keep it businesslike, make it final, and notify the employee of any appeal procedure he or she might follow. Even if you are the appeal procedure, as is likely in an organization that is small, this is still important. Let the employee respond.

▶ Take care of final details. Explain severance pay and insurance procedures. Arrange return of organization keys and other property.

Your objective throughout remains the same: to treat this employee fairly and to show that you have made every reasonable effort to remedy the problem. Do this and you're *probably* legally covered. ("Probably" is italicized as a warning. As mentioned earlier, courts take somewhat erratic views. When in any doubt at all, check with your lawyer.)

## Exit Interview

Exit interviews are a good idea for all departing employees, whether they are leaving voluntarily or not.

| | Excellent | Good | Fair | Poor | Comments |
|---|---|---|---|---|---|
| 1. How were your working conditions? | | | | | |
| 2. How was your compensation? | | | | | |
| 3. How well are employees matched with tasks? | | | | | |
| 4. How well was work organized? | | | | | |
| 5. What did you feel your growth potential was? | | | | | |
| 6. What did you feel your opportunity was to participate, make suggestions, and be involved in your work? | | | | | |
| 7. How was the recognition or credit you received for your contributions? | | | | | |
| 8. How did the managers treat you? | | | | | |
| 9. Can you make any suggestions for making the organization a better place in which to work? | | | | | |
| 10. Remarks: | | | | | |
| Date: | | | | | |
| Forwarding address: | | | | | |
| Organization representative interviewing employee: | | | | | |

**Figure 5-6.** Exit interview

Fill out this form with all departing employees. If the employee is leaving for a better position or a different challenge or retiring voluntarily, this is a good opportunity for you to elicit objective, constructive criticism.

If the separation is not amicable, you should still conduct an exit interview. You give the employee an opportunity to vent his or her anger and a structure for providing specific criticisms. This way, you gain insight into sources of employee dissatisfaction. You also defuse a potentially volatile situation.

# Chapter 6

# Financial Management for Nonprofits 101

*F*INANCIAL MANAGEMENT, THE SECOND MAJOR PIECE OF THE MANAGE-ment puzzle after managing people, deals with the sources and uses of funds, both short and long term. Manage the funds well and the organization will prosper. Manage the funds poorly and disaster lurks.

Setting and using good budgets is 90 percent of financial management. You have to set budgets that reflect your organization and its environments, forecast the changing finances of the organization over time, and apply sufficient financial discipline to keep to the budget.

## Personal Finances

The way you manage your personal finances is financial management on a small scale. Manage carefully and you gain more flexibility in what you might do—buy a better car, send your children to college, take a trip around the world, set money aside for retirement, and so on. You gain a measure of control over your future. But if you don't manage your finances well, chances are good that you will flounder in the muck of financial despair—no savings, poor credit, limited options beyond a panicked response to the most immediate financial crisis.

## Personal Balance Sheet

Start by listing what you own (your assets) and what you owe (your liabilities). The difference between total assets and total liabilities is your net worth. In financial lingo, this list is a balance sheet, a snapshot of your current financial condition.

Put this information into a format based on the formula

$$\text{Assets} - \text{Liabilities} = \text{Net Worth}$$

and you have created a personal balance sheet. Think of this as a two-step process. First, simply list your assets and liabilities. Then arrange the items in each list. List your assets in order of decreasing liquidity, starting with cash and demand deposits and ending with illiquid assets such as real estate. List your liabilities in order of immediacy: bills that have to be paid this week or month down to the final payment of your mortgage (Figure 6-1).

This is similar to a form that many banks require, so it may be familiar. Note that it does not distinguish between short-term (one year or less) and

| Assets | | Liabilities | |
|---|---|---|---|
| Cash (on hand or in banks) | $1,500 | Accounts Payable | $7,000 |
| Savings Accounts | $3,000 | Notes Payable | $5,000 |
| IRA/Other Retirement Funds | $36,000 | Installment Account: Auto | |
| Life Insurance (cash value) | | Installment Account: Other | $500 |
| Stocks and Bonds | $12,000 | Loan on Life Insurance | |
| Real Estate | $240,000 | Mortgages on Real Estate | $120,000 |
| Automobile (current value) | $12,000 | Unpaid Taxes | |
| Other Personal Property | $25,000 | Other Liabilities | $40,000 |
| Other Assets | $30,000 | **Total Liabilities** | **$172,500** |
| | | **Net Worth** | **$187,000** |
| **Total Assets** | **$359,000** | **Total Liabilities + Net Worth** | **$359,000** |

**Figure 6-1.** Personal balance sheet

long-term (more than one year) assets and liabilities. It simply gives a picture of net worth as of a certain date. Compare it with Figure 6-4 below, which is more elaborate but still has the same basic structure.

Net Worth is defined as Total Assets less Total Liabilities.

## Personal Profit and Loss Statement

Most people can anticipate their income and expenses for a year with fair accuracy. The profit and loss statement (P&L) covers a period of time, usually one year. To keep this simple, the example of a personal P&L (Figure 6-2) shows only three months.

| Income | Jan | Feb | Mar | Total |
|---|---|---|---|---|
| Salary (Net of Taxes) | $4,100 | $4,100 | $4,100 | $12,300 |
| Net Investment Income | $200 | $200 | $200 | $600 |
| Real Estate Income | | | | |
| Other Income (Describe Below) | | | | |
| **Total Income** | $4,300 | $4,300 | $4,300 | $12,900 |
| **Expenses** | | | | |
| **Monthly Payments** | | | | |
| Rent or Mortgage | $1,500 | $1,500 | $1,500 | $4,500 |
| Utilities | $400 | $400 | $400 | $1,200 |
| Auto Loan | $225 | $225 | $225 | $675 |
| **Other Monthly Payments** | | | | |
| *Insurance* | | | | |
| Medical | $500 | $500 | $500 | $1,500 |
| Auto | $100 | $100, | $100, | $300, |
| Homeowner's | $335 | $335 | $335 | $1,005 |
| Interest | | | | |
| Other Expense | $210 | $210 | $210 | $630 |
| Household (Food, etc.) | $900 | $900 | $900 | $2,700 |
| **Total Expenses** | $4,270 | $4,270 | $4,270 | $12,810 |
| **Surplus (Deficit)** | $30 | $30 | $30 | $90 |

**Figure 6-2.** Personal profit and loss statement

This personal P&L starts by listing the sources of income: salary, investment, real estate, and other. Total income per month is shown on Line 11. Total expenses are on Line 25. Each month expenses are subtracted from income to show a surplus or deficit for the month. The Statement of Activities (the nonprofit equivalent of the P&L) in Figure 6-8 below is very similar to this example, but much more detailed.

## Personal Cash Flow Budget

Now turn to the ebb and flow of your cash. Pay special heed to timing.

You have a pretty good idea of what cash will be coming in: pay, interest on investments and savings, dividends, tax refunds, and a certificate of deposit coming due. You might even factor in anticipated windfalls: inheritance from an aged aunt, royalties from that screenplay you just sold, sale of a fixed asset (such as a vacation home), and proceeds from a lawsuit. These are clearly one-time items, but they can be substantial.

Now look at the cash going out. You have fixed payments, such as your monthly mortgage and loan payments, utilities, and contributions to your 401(k). Other payments may be scheduled: tuition bills twice a year, that big vacation to Hawaii, and insurance bills four times a year. You also have those ongoing variable bills for food, gas, medical expenses, and so on. These are a little less consistent than the fixed expenses, but you can anticipate them. Tot the inflows and outflows up for each month and for the entire year—and you have created a cash flow budget that will let you know if and when you need to borrow money (Figure 6-3).

That's financial management in a nutshell. No mysteries there. Financial management for an organization is perhaps more detailed but in principle is no different.

Now it becomes murkier. While the P&L showed a surplus of $90 over the same three months, the cash flow budget shows a negative cash flow—a deficit of $2,675. How can this be?

Most of the difference comes from timing issues. In the P&L, income and expenses are shown as incurred, but do not always reflect the timing.

For simplicity, income is the same in both the P&L and the cash flow budget (CF).

For rent or mortgage, the P&L shows $0/month, but the cash flow shows $900. That's because the cash flow shows principal payments separate from interest payments: see Line 23 of the CF, where the interest is displayed separately.

| Source of Income | Jan | Feb | Mar | Total |
|---|---|---|---|---|
| Salary (Net of Taxes) | $4,100 | $4,100 | $4,100 | $12,300 |
| Net Investment Income | $200 | $200 | $200 | $600 |
| Real Estate Income | | | | |
| Other Income (Describe Below) | | | | |
| **Total Income** | $4,300 | $4,300 | $4,300 | $12,900 |
| **Expenses** | | | | |
| **Monthly Payments** | | | | |
| Rent or Mortgage | $900 | $900 | $900 | $2,700 |
| Utilities | $400 | $400 | $400 | $1,200 |
| Auto Loan | $225 | $225 | $225 | $675 |
| Other Monthly Payments | $100 | $100 | $100 | $300 |
| *Insurance*<br> Medical<br> Auto<br> Homeowner's | $1,500 | $1,000 | $1,200<br>$335 | $1,500<br>$1,200<br>$1,000 |
| Interest | $600 | $600 | $600 | $1,800 |
| Other Expense | | $2,500 | | $2,500 |
| Household (Food, etc.) | $800 | $1,100 | $800 | $2,700 |
| **Total Expenses** | $4,525 | $6,825 | $4,225 | $15.575 |
| **Surplus (Deficit)** | −$225 | −$2,525 | $75 | −$2,675 |

**Figure 6-3.** Personal monthly cash flow budget

Look at medical insurance. On the P&L, it shows as $500/month, while in the cash flow, it is shown as $1,500 in January. That's because the premium is due quarterly.

Auto insurance is paid in one $1,200 lump, but shown as $100/month (or $1,200/year) in the P&L. The payment covers the 12 months from March through the following February. The homeowner's policy is also paid once a year (February on the cash flow), thus avoiding additional costs, but is spread over the year at $210/month in the P&L.

The final very variable expense is for a long-awaited trip to Hawaii in February. This is a one-time event, budgeted over a year at $210/month on the P&L. Since food on trips is expensive, an additional $300 is tacked onto the normal $800/month allotted for household expenses on the cash flow.

The value of the cash flow is that it lets you know in advance what disbursements (payments) must be made and when, so that you can plan to have the cash ready to meet those demands. Almost everyone budgets, juggling cash availability against bills or major purchases that can be foreseen. While a major unexpected bill (usually medical, hence the desirability of health insurance) can derail even the most careful budget, it is always better to budget. For your nonprofit, budgeting is even more important: more is at stake.

# Statement of Financial Position, aka Balance Sheet

*Balance sheets for large organizations can be very detailed, but they still have the same form as your personal balance sheet.*

Balance sheets for large organizations can be very detailed, but they still have the same form as your personal balance sheet. Your initial balance sheet will be simple. Look at Figure 6-4. It is not much more complicated than Figure 6-1. Assets and Liabilities are divided into Current and Noncurrent. This allows a quick assessment of the ability of the organization to pay its bills.

A common financial ratio, the *current ratio*, is current assets divided by current liabilities. A current ratio below 2:1 is a red flag. Another key ratio,

| Assets | |
|---|---|
| **Current Assets** | |
| Cash | $2,000 |
| Accounts Receivable | $4,600 |
| Prepaid Expenses | $800 |
| **Total Current Assets** | $7,400 |
| **Noncurrent Assets** | |
| Fixed Assets | $190,000 |
| Grants Receivable | $24,000 |
| **Total Noncurrent Assets** | $214,000 |
| **Total Assets** | $221,400 |

**Figure 6-4.** Statement of financial position (continued on next page)

| Liabilities and Net Assets | |
|---|---|
| **Current Liabilities** | |
| Accounts Payable | $800 |
| Deferred Revenue | $2,200 |
| **Total Current Liabilities** | $3,000 |
| **Noncurrent Liabilities** | |
| Notes Payable | $4,000 |
| Mortgage | $60,000 |
| **Total Noncurrent Liabilities** | $64,000 |
| **Net Assets** | |
| Unrestricted | $31,500 |
| Temporarily Restricted | $16,400 |
| Permanently Restricted | $108,000 |
| Net Income (Loss) YTD | −$1,500 |
| **Total Net Assets** | $154,400 |
| **Total Liabilities and Net Assets** | $221,400 |

**Figure 6-4.** Statement of financial position (continued)

the *acid test*, is cash plus demand deposits divided by current liabilities. (*Demand deposits* are deposits that can be drawn upon instantly, like checking accounts.) An acid test below 1:1 is considered risky.

Grants Receivable are grants due that have not yet been funded, that is, the check hasn't arrived yet. You can't spend that money—hence its place in Noncurrent Assets.

Net Assets are complicated by being dividing into three categories. Unrestricted assets can be used for any legitimate purpose. Temporarily restricted assets carry donor-imposed time restrictions or purpose restrictions. Permanently restricted assets are those with limits established by the donors. The Net Assets category corresponds to Net Worth in a personal or for-profit balance sheet.

Sometimes the Net Assets are called Fund Balance. It is still derived the same way, Total Assets minus Total Liabilities. Figure 6-5 provides an example of a more complex balance sheet.

| Assets | | | Liabilities | | |
|---|---|---|---|---|---|
| **Current Assets** | | | **Current Liabilities** | | |
| Cash | | | Taxes Payable | | |
| Checking Account #1 | $50,000 | | Federal Withholding | $1,500 | |
| Checking Account #2 | $5,000 | | FICA | | |
| Total Cash | $55,000 | | FUTA | | |
| | | | Other (Specify) | | |
| Near Cash | | | Total Taxes Payable | $1,500 | |
| CD#1 | $10,000 | | Notes Payable Long-Term Debt | $35,000 | |
| CD #2 | $22,000 | | | | |
| CD #3 | | | Accounts Payable | $12,500 | |
| Notes Receivable | | | Prepaid Grants | $75,000 | |
| Total Near Cash | $32,000 | | | | |
| Grants Receivable (Specify) | | | Other Liabilities (Specify) | | |
| Accounts Receivable | $11,500 | | **Total Current Liabilities** | $124,000 | |
| Prepaid Expenses | | | Long-Term Liabilities | | |
| **Total Current Assets** | $98,500 | | Long-Term Debt | $325,000 | |
| **Fixed Assets** | | | Other Long-Term Liabilities (Specify) | | |
| Plant | $300,000 | | | | |
| Equipment | $35,000 | | **Total Long-Term Liabilities** | $325,000 | |
| Encumbered Capital | $125,000 | | **Fund Balance** | $109,000 | |
| **Total Fixed Assets** | $460,000 | | **Total Liabilities and Fund Balance** | $558,500 | |
| **Total Assets** | $558,500 | | | | |

**Figure 6-5.** Complex statement of financial position

Note that the current ratio and the acid test for this nonprofit are both in dangerous territory. In this instance a major successful fund drive had not yet delivered its bounty and a number of grant applications were awaiting decisions. The board members panicked when they saw this monthly balance sheet. Their fears were mollified by the treasurer's assurance that the drive had raised nearly $200,000 and a number of grants had been verbally approved though official word had not yet arrived. This is by no means uncommon. Timing is always important in understanding financial statements.

# Statement of Activities, aka Nonprofit P&L or Income Statement

Look at the statement of activities (Figure 6-6). It differs very little from the personal P&L (Figure 6-2). It shows the income for the period (in this case for three years projected out), the expenses, and the difference between the two. These numbers are rounded up from an actual pro forma P&L.

| Statement of Activities | 2008 | 2009 | 2010 |
|---|---|---|---|
| Foundation, Corporate, and Private Support | $700,000 | $450,000 | $700,000 |
| Public Funds | $500,000 | $725,000 | $925,000 |
| Fees for Service | $100,000 | $275,000 | $325,000 |
| Total Support | $1,300,000 | $1,450,000 | $1,950,000 |
| Expenses | | | |
| Program Service | $1,000,000 | $1,300,000 | $1,500,000 |
| Management and General | $200,000 | $250,000 | $275,000 |
| Fundraising | $40,000 | $50,000 | $60,000 |
| Total Expenses | $1,240,000 | $1,600,000 | $1,835,000 |
| Increase (Decrease) in Net Assets | $60,000 | −$150,000 | $115,000 |
| Beginning Net Assets | $350,000 | $410,000 | $260,000 |
| Ending Net Assets | $410,000 | $260,000 | $375,000 |

Figure 6-6. Statement of activities

## Pro-forma Statements

Financial statements that depict a future period are called *pro-forma* or *projected* financial statements. They represent what the organization is expected to look like financially, based on a set of assumptions about the economy, market growth, and other factors.

Income projections are forecasting and budgeting tools estimating income and anticipating expenses in the near to middle-range future. For most organizations (and for most bankers) income projections covering one to three years are more than adequate. In some cases, a longer projection may be called for, but in general, the longer the projection, the less accurate it will be as a guide to action.

Not too complex. But then look at the Figure 6-7, in which all the details were broken out by month. The point? The level of detail you want to show in your monthly and annual statements of activities depends on what you, your accountant, and your treasurer think is necessary. However, in your nonprofit's books, all of this detail and more will be needed.

| Support | Jan | Feb | Mar | Apr | May | Jun |
|---|---|---|---|---|---|---|
| *Grforms*<br>HCTGII<br>HCTGIII<br>CNS III Providian<br>Eisenhower<br>CDBG<br>NHCF<br>Special Needs<br>BSAS<br>HCGT V | | | | | | |
| ***Total Public Funds*** | $ | $ | $ | $ | $ | $ |
| *Fundraising*<br>Corporate Fairs<br>Individuals | | | | | | |
| ***Total Foundation, Corporate, and Private Support*** | $ | $ | $ | $ | $ | $ |
| *Fee for Service*<br>VISTA<br>Expertise<br>#1<br>#2<br>#3<br>#4<br>#%<br>Americorps | | | | | | |
| ***Total Fee for Service*** | $ | $ | $ | $ | $ | $ |
| *Interest Income* | | | | | | |
| ***Total Interest Income*** | $ | $ | $ | $ | $ | $ |
| **Total Support** | $ | $ | $ | $ | $ | $ |

**Figure 6-7.** Complex P&L material (continued on next page)

| Expenses | Jan | Feb | Mar | Apr | May | Jun |
|---|---|---|---|---|---|---|
| Adjust for Administration and Overhead (see notes) | | | | | | |
| VISTA Stipends<br>VISTA FICA<br>Americorps Stipends<br>Americorps Benefits<br>Postage<br>Office Supplies/Equipment<br>Staff Development<br>Auto and Travel<br>Meetings<br>Dues and Subscriptions<br>Rent and Occupancy<br>Dover Program<br>Telephone<br>Special Events<br>Relocation<br>Miscellaneous<br>Other Accounts<br>Purchased Services<br>  Printing<br>  Library<br>  Mini-grants<br>  Conference | | | | | | |
| *Total* | $ | $ | $ | $ | $ | $ |
| *Administration and Overhead*<br>  L&A<br>  Consulting<br>  Insurance<br>  Interest<br>  Postage<br>  Telephone<br>  Rent and Occupancy<br>  Salaries and Benefits | | | | | | |
| *Total A&O* | $ | $ | $ | $ | $ | $ |
| *Loan Repayments* | | | | | | |
| *Total Loan Repayments* | $ | $ | $ | $ | $ | $ |

**Figure 6-7.** Complex P&L material (continued on next page)

| | Jan | Feb | Mar | Apr | May | Jun |
|---|---|---|---|---|---|---|
| **Total Expenses** | $ | $ | $ | $ | $ | $ |
| *Increase (Decrease) Net Assets* | $ | $ | $ | $ | $ | $ |
| *Beginning Net Assets* | $ | $ | $ | $ | $ | $ |
| *Ending Net Assets* | $ | $ | $ | $ | $ | $ |

**Figure 6-7.** Complex P&L material (continued)

# Forecast Revenues

*Projecting revenues is more art than science; at best it will be an imprecise affair.*

Projecting revenues is more art than science; at best it will be an imprecise affair. Too many outside factors affect revenues: economic conditions, competition, changes in grant and donor patterns, even the weather. But you still have to estimate the level of revenue your organization will strive to reach. Once your NPO is up and running, your ideas will be corrected by experience. But now, the most you can hope for is to provide educated guesses based on your ideas, your research, and industry figures such as those provided by GuideStar.org (*www.guidestar.org*).

You will use the revenue forecast in both the projected P&L and in your cash flow projection.

The simplest way to project revenues is to take a "worst case, best case, most likely case" approach. For a start-up, this is even more difficult than for a going organization since you don't have historical figures to guide your projections (Figure 6-8).

| Source | Worst Case | Most Likely Case | Best Case |
|---|---|---|---|
| A. | | | |
| B. | | | |
| C. | | | |
| D. | | | |
| E. | | | |
| **Total** | | | |

**Figure 6-8.** Projecting revenue from various sources

Break your revenue sources down into small chunks. You may be planning to apply for funds from several sources (individual donors, foundations, grants) and charging a fee for service. After estimating the gross revenue figures in the worst- and best-case scenarios, choose an in-between figure for most likely. Total the figures in the Most Likely Case column and spread it over the 12 months of the cash flow projection for the first year.

## Income and Cash Flow Forecasting

Small NPOs should make three-year projections for planning purposes and loan proposals. Here's the proper sequence for both income and cash flow projections:

1. A three-year summary.
2. First year projected by month. If the business doesn't break even in the first year, you might want to continue the monthly projections until it does.
3. Years Two and Three by quarter.

If you are already in business, include historical financial statements for two immediately previous years. Tax returns help to substantiate the validity of unaudited statements.

Remember that these figures are educated guesses. As you gain experience, your guesses will become more educated and more accurate. If you err, try to err on the conservative side. If you estimate revenues lower than they turn out to be, you'll be better off than pitching your estimate too high. Why? Because some expenses are geared to the revenue forecast, and it is always easier to spend more than to save or cut back.

# Project Your Cash Flow

Start with the easy part. Fixed monthly payments can be figured accurately. These include rent, salaries and benefits, equipment rental payments, and any monthly term-loan payment. Payments that aren't made monthly, but whose size and timing can be scheduled, come next. Ongoing advertising and marketing disbursements, some loan payments, and equipment purchases are examples. Predictable payments are largely discretionary, though some are necessary but sporadic (licenses, for example). You have considerable choice over when to make most of these payments and will use these opportunities to juggle your cash flow.

Now turn to cash inflow. Using your "most likely" revenue forecasts, try to spread out cash from all revenue sources plus cash from receivables over the year. Each month will probably be different, depending on the season. Seasonal patterns have a dramatic effect on the shape of cash flows. You should seek out advice on the patterns you will most likely face. Consider the black-out period when the United Way is seeking its funding. Consider the impact of taxes on individual donors' giving patterns. Ask your peers.

Variable payments depend on the level of activities. If you will be using part-time or contract help at various times, reflect this in your budget.

For taxes, ask your accountant for help. Taxes are part of the cost of doing business: if you make money, you have to pay taxes. Most nonprofits avoid "unrelated business income taxes," but it is best to be sure. Their timing and amount vary—not at your whim but at the behest of the IRS.

At this point, you can make the first cut at your cash flow. (It will change after you add back capital investment and proceeds from loans.) Figure the cash flow for each month: net cash flow equals total cash inflows minus total cash outflows.

Now calculate cumulative cash flow for the entire first year. If it continues steadily downhill, keep projecting until the cumulative cash flow definitely begins to turn up toward a positive figure. (If it never turns up, don't start unless your advisors can show you where your numbers have gone wrong.) For the first month, cumulative cash flow equals net cash flow. For the second month and beyond, add the new month's net cash flow to the previous month's cumulative cash flow to arrive at the new month's cumulative cash flow.

You can now calculate how much capital your organization needs (start-up capital plus bank or other debt).

Some cash inflows have to be postponed. The reason is that in almost every start-up there are negative cash flows from the beginning because revenues take a while to develop, while expenses start immediately. You will have to use inflows from new capital and loan proceeds to cover these negative cash flows. Look for the lowest cumulative cash flow in your projection. Double that figure to arrive at the capital your organization will need. Money won't come in as fast as you hope—and you can bet on it going out faster than you feel comfortable with. The timing and amount of cash inflows needed from new capital and proceeds of loans can now be figured. The amount of cash from capital and loan proceeds should be spread out over the cash flow projection as needed. As a rule, capital comes in first. Then aim to borrow only as you must.

Meet with your banker for preliminary talks whether or not you will use bank credit. Your banker will help calculate your borrowing needs if you ask. Bring your cash flow statement and you will also establish your credibility in his or her eyes. To minimize your costs, minimize borrowing. Use your cash flow projection to show your banker how much money you need, when, how you will pay it back, and why it is a good investment of the bank's money.

# Budget Deviation: Putting the Budget to Work

The simplest way to use a budget is to set up a form at the beginning of the month that has your projected figures in one column and actual figures in the other. At the end of the month, compare the two columns. If disbursements are down, find out why. It's easy to miss a payment or reduce inventory without reordering. If disbursements are up, find out why. You may have prepaid a bill or overstocked. Then check inflows the same way. Look for variations; then seek the cause. That's **budget deviation analysis** (BDA).

To be effective, run a BDA at least monthly. If you have several concurrent projects, you might want to devise separate budgets and deviation analyses for each project. Done properly, BDA will tell you at a glance which parts of your organization are out of control and which ones are exceeding expectations.

*Done properly, budget deviation analysis will tell you at a glance which parts of your organization are out of control and which ones are exceeding expectations.*

Modify the BDA forms on the following pages to suit the particular needs of your nonprofit. Columns C and D are derived from actual and budgeted figures. Experience will tell you which deviations—and of what magnitude—are significant. Examine any deviation, positive or negative, and understand the reasons for it. Next, take corrective action (if the deviation is working against you) or exploit the serendipitous improvement in performance (if the deviation is in your favor).

For example, suppose that utilities, budgeted for $600 in January, actually cost $1,340. Why? The weather was exceptionally cold, insulation was not installed until the end of the month, and you will replace a broken skylight as soon as possible. If close attention had not been paid to the utility bill, that cost could easily have gotten out of hand. Suppose that client fees were $18,000 in January, not the anticipated (budgeted) $14,600. What went right? Careful attention to a positive deviation can pay off in greatly increased revenues.

117

Year-to-date BDA is another good financial tool. If more expenditures fall in one month than were expected, you will find a corresponding lowering of expenditures the preceding or following month. The year-to-date BDA helps to level out these swings. Used with the monthly BDAs, this form will save you some unnecessary arithmetic and worry, as well as check the accuracy and effectiveness of your projections. With experience, your budgeting will become more exact, affording you greater control over your business and profits.

As with the other control documents, you should adapt the suggested formats that follow to fit your business needs. Your accountant should help with this—but you have to be the person who decides what information should be reflected by BDA. Ask your accountant to help. Add information only if you can check it out against actual performance, which will often call for professional expertise. You have an organization to run, after all, which is why you hire accountants rather than become one yourself. (See Figures 6-9 to 6-12.)

| | A<br>Actual for<br>Month | B<br>Budget for<br>Month | C<br>Deviation<br>(B – A) | D<br>% Deviation<br>C/B x 100) |
|---|---|---|---|---|
| **Revenues**<br>Foundation, Corporate, and<br>Private<br>Public<br>Fees for Service | | | | |
| **Sales** | | | | |
| **Less Cost of Goods Sold** | | | | |
| **Gross Profit on Sales** | | | | |
| **Operating Expenses**<br>*Variable Expenses*<br>Contract Labor<br>Advertising<br>Miscellaneous Variable<br>*Total Variable Expenses*<br>*Fixed Expenses*<br>Utilities<br>Salaries<br>Payroll Taxes and Benefits<br>Office Supplies<br>Insurance<br>Maintenance and Cleaning | | | | |

**Figure 6-9.** Budget deviation analysis by month (continued on next page)

| | A Actual for Month | B Budget for Month | C Deviation (B – A) | D % Deviation C/B x 100 |
|---|---|---|---|---|
| **Operating Expenses (continued)** | | | | |
|   Legal and Accounting | | | | |
|   Delivery | | | | |
|   Licenses | | | | |
|   Telephone | | | | |
|   Miscellaneous | | | | |
|   Depreciation | | | | |
|   Interest | | | | |
| *Total Fixed Expenses* | | | | |
| **Total Operating Expenses** | | | | |
| **Increase (Decrease) Net Assets** | | | | |

**Figure 6-9.** Budget deviation analysis by month (continued)

**From the Statement of Activities Year-to-Date** _____

| | A Actual for Month | B Budget for Month | C Deviation (B – A) | D % Deviation C/B x 100 |
|---|---|---|---|---|
| **Revenues** | | | | |
|   Foundation, Corporate, and Private | | | | |
|   Public | | | | |
|   Fees for Service | | | | |
| **Sales** | | | | |
| **Less Cost of Goods Sold** | | | | |
| **Gross Profit on Sales** | | | | |
| **Operating Expenses** | | | | |
|   *Variable Expenses* | | | | |
|     Contract Labor | | | | |
|     Advertising | | | | |
|     Miscellaneous Variable | | | | |
|   *Total Variable Expenses* | | | | |

**Figure 6-10.** Budget deviation analysis year-to-date (continued on next page)

**From the Statement of Activities Year-to-Date** _____

| | A<br>Actual for<br>Month | B<br>Budget for<br>Month | C<br>Deviation<br>(B − A) | D<br>% Deviation<br>C/B x 100) |
|---|---|---|---|---|
| **Operating Expenses (continued)** | | | | |
| _Fixed Expenses_ | | | | |
| Utilities | | | | |
| Salaries | | | | |
| Payroll Taxes and Benefits | | | | |
| Office Supplies | | | | |
| Insurance | | | | |
| Maintenance and Cleaning | | | | |
| Legal and Accounting | | | | |
| Delivery | | | | |
| Licenses | | | | |
| Telephone | | | | |
| Miscellaneous | | | | |
| Depreciation | | | | |
| Interest | | | | |
| _Total Fixed Expenses_ | | | | |
| **Total Operating Expenses** | | | | |
| **Increase (Decrease) Net Assets** | | | | |

**Figure 6-10.** Budget deviation analysis year-to-date (continued)

**From the Cash Flow Pro Forma for the Month of** _____

| | A<br>Actual for<br>Month | B<br>Budget for<br>Month | C<br>Deviation<br>(B − A) | D<br>% Deviation<br>C/B x 100) |
|---|---|---|---|---|
| **Beginning Cash Balance** | | | | |
| **Add:** | | | | |
| Increase (Decrease) in Net Assets | | | | |
| Cash Sales | | | | |
| Accounts Receivable That Have Turned to Cash | | | | |
| Other Case Inflows | | | | |
| **Total Available Cash** | | | | |

**Figure 6-11.** Budget deviation analysis by month (continued on next page)

**From the Cash Flow Pro Forma for the Month of** _____

| | A<br>Actual for Month | B<br>Budget for Month | C<br>Deviation (B – A) | D<br>% Deviation C/B x 100) |
|---|---|---|---|---|
| **Deduct Estimated Disbursements:** | | | | |
| Cost of Materials | | | | |
| Contract Labor | | | | |
| Advertising | | | | |
| Insurance | | | | |
| Legal and Accounting | | | | |
| Delivery | | | | |
| Equipment* | | | | |
| Loan Payments | | | | |
| Mortgage Payment | | | | |
| Property Tax Expense | | | | |
| **Deduct Fixed Cash Disbursements:** | | | | |
| Utilities | | | | |
| Salaries | | | | |
| Payroll Taxes and Benefits | | | | |
| Office Supplies | | | | |
| Maintenance and Cleaning | | | | |
| Licenses | | | | |
| Telephone | | | | |
| Miscellaneous | | | | |
| **Total Disbursements** | | | | |
| **Ending Cash Balance** | | | | |

*Equipment expense represents actual expenditures made for purchase of equipment.

**Figure 6-11.** Budget deviation analysis by month (continued)

You will also notice that "Column D: % Deviation" will magnify small numbers. If Maintenance and Cleaning is budgeted at $25/month and comes in at $50, the percentage deviation is 100 percent. This is deliberate. Large dollar deviations show up clearly in "Column C: Deviation," but small deviations can collectively become fairly large and have a devastating cumulative effect on profits. This is another area where a bit of computer power takes the drudgery (and opportunities for error) out of repetitive monthly calculations. Set your tolerances. Then follow up on all significant deviations.

**Budget Deviation Analysis Year-to-Date From the Cash Flow Year-to-Date** _____

|  | A<br>Actual for<br>Month | B<br>Budget for<br>Month | C<br>Deviation<br>(B − A) | D<br>% Deviation<br>C/B x 100) |
|---|---|---|---|---|
| **Beginning Cash Balance** |  |  |  |  |
| **Add:** |  |  |  |  |
| Increase (Decrease) in Net Assets |  |  |  |  |
| Cash Sales |  |  |  |  |
| Accounts Receivable That Have Turned to Cash |  |  |  |  |
| Other Cash Inflows |  |  |  |  |
| Sales Revenue |  |  |  |  |
| Other Revenue |  |  |  |  |
| **Total Available Cash** |  |  |  |  |
| **Deduct Estimated Disbursements:** |  |  |  |  |
| Cost of Materials |  |  |  |  |
| Contract Labor |  |  |  |  |
| Advertising |  |  |  |  |
| Insurance |  |  |  |  |
| Legal and Accounting |  |  |  |  |
| Delivery |  |  |  |  |
| Equipment* |  |  |  |  |
| Loan Payments |  |  |  |  |
| Mortgage Payment |  |  |  |  |
| Property Tax Expense |  |  |  |  |
| **Deduct Fixed Cash Disbursements:** |  |  |  |  |
| Disbursements: |  |  |  |  |
| Utilities |  |  |  |  |
| Salaries |  |  |  |  |
| Payroll Taxes and Benefits |  |  |  |  |
| Office Supplies |  |  |  |  |
| Maintenance and Cleaning |  |  |  |  |
| Licenses |  |  |  |  |
| Telephone |  |  |  |  |
| Miscellaneous |  |  |  |  |

**Figure 6-12.** Budget Deviation Analysis Year-to-Date (continued on next page)

**Budget Deviation Analysis Year-to-Date From the Cash Flow Year-to-Date** _____

|  | A<br>Actual for<br>Month | B<br>Budget for<br>Month | C<br>Deviation<br>(B – A) | D<br>% Deviation<br>C/B x 100) |
|---|---|---|---|---|
| **Total Disbursements** |  |  |  |  |
| **Ending Cash Balance** |  |  |  |  |

**Calculations:**
A. Add current month actual to last month's year-to-date analysis.
B. Add current month budget to last month's year-to-date analysis.
*Equipment expense represents actual expenditures made for purchase of equipment.

**Figure 6-12.** Budget Deviation Analysis Year-to-Date (continued)

HELP
HERE

# Chapter 7

# Strategic Planning

**M**OST NONPROFITS USE A STRATEGIC PLANNING PROCESS TO identify and agree on the strategies that will guide their organization over the long haul, usually five years or longer.

## What Is a Strategic Plan?

A strategic plan systematically sets goals and objectives that, if achieved, will further the mission of the organization. Within the contexts set by the strategic plan, the business plan (which looks forward one to three years) takes a more tactical approach.

Schematically:

strategic plan ➔ long-term goals and objectives ➔ tactical or
business plan ➔ specific steps to achieve those goals and objectives

Do you need a strategic plan? Yes. If you don't work out a strategic plan, you adopt a strategy of being reactive and trusting to luck. Write down the plan so you can refer to it later. Plan to revisit and rethink the plan at least every two years.

The *process* of planning (for both strategic and business plans) is valuable in and of itself. If you follow the process (and keep notes), your nonprofit will become stronger, its volunteers, staff, and board will become more closely aligned to the mission, and morale will benefit. Remember that the most important part of management is managing people. It's an educational process that provides a forum for interaction and communication.

# Who Should Be Involved in Strategic Planning?

Start the strategic plan with your executive committee, to provide a base. Ideally you will then involve staff, some clients, and perhaps a few other stakeholders in working through the seven steps.

Why involve so many people? Simple. You want to achieve buy-in from all parties. Reviewing the mission gets people on the same page; discussing each step creates ownership of the resultant goals. A strategic plan sent down from above runs the danger of resistance, if not anger, from those below. More to the point, the people who are on the front line every day will have insights and ideas that the executive committee can't have. That day-to-day experience and the wider purview of the board make a powerful combination, rooted in reality and aware of the possibilities the organization might achieve.

The role of consultants (facilitators, trainers, outside nonprofit experts) in strategic planning is open to question. Some people think the value of an outsider lies in that an outsider is more disinterested and more objective than any insider, whether staff or board. It also is easier for staff to speak their minds without worrying about organizational politics. The downside is that consultants have to be paid. If cash is short, there may be other resources to facilitate meetings. Ask the United Way in your area for help. They may have a list of unpaid consultants (retired executives, for instance) who give back to their community in this way.

*The role of consultants (facilitators, trainers, outside nonprofit experts) in strategic planning is open to question.*

# How Do You Approach Strategic Planning?

Strategic planning follows a logical pattern, step by step:

1. Revisit the mission statement, updating it as needed.
2. List the four or five most significant strengths. Then do the same for weaknesses, opportunities, and threats.

125

3. List the most pressing weaknesses and threats, strengths and opportunities.
4. Build on strengths and opportunities; shore up or obviate weaknesses and threats. This is the heart of strategic planning.
5. Express the goals in measurable terms.
6. Turn the goals (long term) into objectives (short term).

The goals and objectives should be SMART: *s*pecific, *m*easurable, *a*ttainable, *r*ealistic, and *t*imed. The strategic planning process guarantees (well, almost!) that the organization focuses on its most important activities and that all plans lead to achieving the same set of long-term goals.

## Step 1: Revisit the Mission Statement

One of the dangers in strategic planning is getting hung up on the first step, revisiting and revising the mission statement. Some experts recommend keeping this step separate, perhaps with a meeting for the mission statement alone, and reaching agreement on the mission before going forward. Others say that you can do both, that revising and rephrasing the mission is appropriate at any time. If you cannot achieve consensus on the mission before you proceed to step two and beyond, you'll just waste time.

Before the first meeting of the strategic planning committee (executive committee, ED, key staff, and other stakeholders), give the members all a copy of your current mission statement. Ask them to review it, paying special attention to the following questions:

1. Does it reflect the purpose of the organization?
2. Has the purpose changed (for whatever reason) enough to rewrite the mission statement?
3. Do new programs or services stretch the mission statement?
4. If a new revision is in order, what changes do you suggest?

Collect the responses, collate them, and come to the first meeting with the new statement. If you decide to keep the old one, be prepared to offer reasons why it should be retained.

## Step 2: Make a SWOT List

List the most significant strengths, weaknesses, opportunities, and threats. Take these one by one, beginning with strengths and weaknesses.

Start with the internal environment, which is limited to factors you can directly control. Internal strengths might be quality of staff, service delivery, operations, and financial resources. These might also be weaknesses; it may be that one item is both a strength and a weakness.

This is where you must begin to include staff and stakeholders. Their perceptions of what is good or bad about internal operations may differ. Fine. This is valuable information. Use whatever technique you can think of to elicit ideas: self-adhesive slips are popular. (Give each person a pad of slips so they can write down their ideas. Summarize and post the notes under the categories you choose as summary. This provides you some control.) You are not seeking consensus—but you do want everyone to have his or her say. The agreement you want to seek is that the list contains the most important strengths and the most distressing weaknesses.

| Factor | Strengths | Weakness |
|--------|-----------|----------|
| 1.     |           |          |
| 2.     |           |          |
| 3.     |           |          |
| 4.     |           |          |
| 5.     |           |          |

**Figure 7-1.** Internal strengths and weaknesses

Limit your list to no more than five strengths and five weaknesses. If you only have one or two, that's OK. Now list them on Figure 7-1.

Use the same approach for the external environment, to identify opportunities and threats. What outside forces, the ones that you cannot control, will likely affect your organization over the next couple of years? Think, for example, of the impact of the general economy (good or bad), legal changes, demographic shifts, technological advances, or competition.

Again, limit your list to five opportunities and five threats. Focus on the big items, the proverbial low-hanging fruit. Open the way for discussion, keep notes, and fill in Figure 7-2. Do not feel you must have five of each—perhaps one opportunity is so huge that it will consume all of your efforts or one threat is so frightening that the survival of the NPO is threatened.

| Factor | Opportunity | Threat |
|---|---|---|
| 1. | | |
| 2. | | |
| 3. | | |
| 4. | | |
| 5. | | |

**Figure 7-2.** External opportunities and threats

## Step 3: Identify the Most Important Factors

Keep this short. Think of this as a winnowing process. A successful strategy is one that addresses the most critical factors. Identifying those factors is often the messiest part of the process, since people will hold strong opinions on what is important.

At this point break out the self-adhesive slips again. You have two concerns. First, which factors are the most important? Second, how do you rank them? Be prepared for a lot of discussion. Note that the focus now shifts to identifying the most important strengths and best opportunities (you want to build on these) on the one hand and the most dire weaknesses and threats on the other (you want to find a way to mitigate these).

After sufficient discussion, fill in Figure 7-3. You decide what constitutes "sufficient discussion." You want everyone to be heard, another argument in favor of post-its as an augmentation to discussion. Some people are shy and won't speak out—but will jot down their ideas.

Don't feel that you have to have five items on each list. Limit each list to the most important items and rank-order them from most important to less important.

## Step 4: Plan Action

And now the rubber meets the road. Now you begin to benefit from the strategic planning process.

Take the two most important strengths and opportunities and the two most important weaknesses and threats. Why limit it to two? Simple. Your resources and capabilities are limited and you want to focus your efforts on

| Our most important strengths and best opportunities are: |
| 1. |
| 2. |
| 3. |
| 4. |
| 5. |
| Our most dangerous weaknesses and threats are: |
| 1. |
| 2. |
| 3. |
| 4. |
| 5. |

**Figure 7-3.** Top SWOT list

those items that have the greatest potential for good or ill. You can't focus on five or ten objectives. You can focus on one or two.

This step may reopen discussions about what criteria to use to decide what is "most important" or "most critical." This is healthy; if you don't get some argument here, something is wrong. Ask for input. Demand input. The winnowing process is bound to step on some toes.

Two things are important here. First, seek agreement on what to include as strengths and opportunities. The process is open and inclusive, but the buck stops with you. Second, once the filtering part is done, open up the floor to suggestions about what actions might be taken. Don't expect this to be easy or mechanical.

| 1. Strength or Opportunity<br>Action: |
| 2. Strength or Opportunity<br>Action: |

**Figure 7-4.** Building on strengths and opportunities

To build on our major strengths and opportunities listed on Figure 7-3, fill in Figure 7-4 and plan to take the actions you decide on.

Now you and your fellow strategic planners turn your attention to weaknesses and threats. This discussion will also be contentious, but if you do not allow frank and open discussion, your staff, board members, and other stakeholders won't fully buy in. Remember: managing people is never easy.

After the discussion, fill in Figure 7-5 and decide to take the actions you listed to shore up the major weaknesses and avoid the major threats listed on Figure 7-3.

| 1. Weakness or Threat<br>Action: |
| --- |
| 2. Weakness or Threat<br>Action: |

**Figure 7-5.** Shoring up weaknesses and avoiding threats

## Step 5: Express the Goals in Measurable Terms

Express the goals (long-term objectives) in measurable terms (dollars raised, programs offered, persons hired, alliances, or whatever). Assign responsibility for attaining each goal to a specific person. (If you do not, the odds are nobody will take responsibility.) Assign a due date to each goal. Some may be way out there (five to ten years) while others may be short-term (Figure 7-6).

The point of a strategic plan is to produce focused actions that promote the mission of the organization. The long winnowing process set up the actions agreed on in Step 4; now it is time to make concrete suggestions.

Keep your team involved, especially the members who will be doing the work.

You have defined four or fewer goals as actions in Step 4. How can your organization best achieve those goals, given the restrictions of staff and cash that you face?

Goal 1 is the most important. Goal 2 is second most important. Goals 3 and 4 are third and fourth respectively. This is the final rank ordering in the strategic plan, so once again get as many people involved as you can. The

| Goal 1 |
|---|
| Person responsible: |
| Due date: |
| |
| Goal 2 |
| Person responsible: |
| Due date: |
| |
| Goal 3 |
| Person responsible: |
| Due date: |
| |
| Goal 4 |
| Person responsible: |
| Due date: |
| |

**Figure 7-6.** Long-term goals

different perspectives your team members bring to this task are very valuable in ensuring that you identify the proper goals and **persons.**

## Step 6: Turn the Goals (Long Term) into Objectives (Short Term)

Take one more step and specify what actions you will take over the next one to three years. The long-term goals govern this: objectives are the short-term goals that, as you achieve them, lead you to achieving the long-term goals.

This is an optional step in the strategic planning process, since you will be spelling out the tactical measures for the next year in the business plan (next chapter). What do you have to do in the next year to get closer to reaching your goals?

This quasi-linear process—you look at the goal and work backwards, while at the same time you look at what you have and work forward toward the goal—might be most effective separate from the strategic plan.

| |
|---|
| Long-term Goal 1<br>Short-term objectives: |
| Long-term Goal 2<br>Short-term objectives: |
| Long-term Goal 3<br>Short-term objectives: |
| Long-term Goal 4<br>Short-term objectives: |

**Figure 7-7**. Turning goals into objectives

If you want to assemble a formal strategic plan, you now have all the major pieces. You began with the mission, looked at the organization from inside and out, narrowed down the SWOT, and specified goals to achieve the purpose or mission of the organization. That's all there is to strategic planning.

HELP
HERE

# Chapter 8

# Business Planning

**A**LL NONPROFITS NEED BUSINESS PLANS. *THERE ARE NO EXCEPTIONS.* Business plans give you a chance to test your ideas, understand the way your organization works, try out different scenarios, communicate with the rest of the world (especially funders and bankers), and spell out the financial implications of proposed actions.

You will be able to use some of the work you did in preceding chapters. If you didn't do the work then, OK. You can do it now.

## What Is a Business Plan?

A business plan is a short document (as short as six to 20 pages: for small organizations very few good plans are longer) that sets out the tactical steps to reach the one- to three-year goals outlined in the strategic plan. It includes a description of the organization and its resources and a set of financial projections based on the assumptions contained in the description.

You can write a pretty fair business plan in a weekend. Getting beyond that "pretty fair" will take experience and paying attention to what is happening. No plan is 100-percent accurate (predicting the future is notably difficult), but a carefully thought out plan will be a better guide to the future than some vague "it's in my head" kind of plan.

# Why Do You Need a Business Plan?

There are several reasons for a business plan. One is to please your funders, who are increasingly interested in seeing business plans with measurable results. A plan provides a way to measure progress toward your goals. It is the base for objective and measurable outcomes that charitable foundations and agencies such as the United Way are now demanding. No measurable outcomes? Then no money.

You can use your business plan to model the results of the many decisions you have to make in a changing environment. What if you add an employee? What will the financial impact be—not just for the hire but also for overhead, effect on the ED and other staff, delivery of service, and so on? You can examine the risks of various scenarios. What if giving is down? What if demand for your services grows more quickly than expected? What if you move to more expensive facilities to be closer to your clients?

This "what if" testing is cheap insurance. Bright ideas (hunch-based, as a rule) can be tested before you commit scarce resources and, if the results look risky, you'll lose nothing but a little time.

*You will find that the planning process teaches you a great deal about running your organization and how to improve its prospects.*

You will find that the planning process teaches you a great deal about running your organization and how to improve its prospects. This alone justifies the time and effort business planning takes.

# Nonprofit Business Plan Sketch

Welcome to business planning. This may be an unfamiliar activity for you. Don't worry. Business planning is not only simple and manageable—it can be fun. It certainly will help you with the three most important disciplines involved in running a nonprofit:

1. *Focus* on your clients and markets at all times.
2. Set and pursue clear and realistic *goals*.
3. *Budget* carefully—and follow your budget.

These worksheets will help you get over the biggest planning barrier: the blank sheet of paper. Write your plan in discrete chunks first: fill in the blanks with rough, sketchy answers. You can always go back and rethink an element of your plan or make a substantial change. That's part of the value of a business plan; it gives you a working model of your business idea so you can try out ideas inexpensively.

Your business plan should be *short*. Long plans gather dust. Short plans get used, improved, altered to reflect changes in the environments your business works within.

It must be *written*. As Lao-Tse put it, the finest memory is not so firm as faded ink. You will juggle hundreds of ideas and variables during the planning process and goodness knows how many more once you begin to test the plan in your organization.

Your business plan will help you only if you use it—*plans are tools*. The more carefully you plan (within reason), the better the results. You will gain the best results if you use your plan as a guide to action and decision-making. It is not a straitjacket any more than a set of blueprints or a recipe might be.

Use a *three-ring binder*. Your plan will change, but you will want to keep your earlier ideas for reference and review. A three-ring binder simplifies this record-keeping. Computers are fine, but if you print out your plan and put the parts into a binder, you can leaf through it, make marginal notes, and retain early ideas and drafts.

Your business plan stands on three legs: concept, customers, and cash. While there are refinements that apply to each of these, your plan will be OK if you develop a clear sense of your organization's mission and history (*concept*), if you know who your clients are and why they use your services and programs or support your organization with resources of time, cash, and talent (*customers*)—and if you have enough financial resources to afford to serve those markets (*cash*).

*Your business plan stands on three legs: concept, customers, and cash.*

For some new or proposed NPOs, this business plan sketch is all that is really needed. For others, the sketch is just a beginning. As the organization grows, however, a full business plan (see below) will provide the best bang for the buck.

To sketch out your business plan, briefly answer the following questions.

**Concept:**

▶ *What business are you in?* What are the purpose and mission and/or vision that drive the organization?

▶ *What are your services, programs, and products?* Describe them.

▶ *What benefits do your services, programs, and products provide your clients and prospects?*

▶ *How do these benefits impact the community?*

▶ *What are the measurable outcomes or what will the measurable outcomes be?*

**Customers:**

▶ *Who are the people in your target markets?*

▶ *What benefits do they seek from you?*

▶ *Promotion: How (and what) do they know about your organization?*

▶ *Competition: Who are your leading competitors?*

▶ *What do your competitors do better than you? Worse than you?*

▶ *What is your location?* Why did you choose it?

▶ *When are you open?*

▶ *Management: Who is in charge?*

▶ *What are your personnel needs?*

▶ *Who are your outside advisors?*

**Cash:**

▶ *What are your projected revenues for the next year?*

▶ *How much capital do you need to meet your service and social goals?*

▶ *How much debt can you safely carry?*

▶ *What does your* cash flow pro forma *tell you?*

## Questions to Ask Your Financial Advisors

1. How do you establish an effective *cash flow budget?*
2. How can you reach and/or maintain a positive cash flow?
3. What is this NPO's breakeven point?
4. How does your organization compare with similar organizations?
5. How much money do you need to borrow and when?
6. How do you know you are generating sufficient revenue to maintain your organization?
7. Can you afford to do this?
8. Should you try to build revenues, cut costs, or both?

# Sample Nonprofit Business Plan Format

Few topics have been more thoroughly examined than business planning. Google "business planning" and spend the rest of your life looking at over 736,000,000 hits! Almost every business planning book or software program has its own format for business plans. You might benefit from checking out several formats, one of which might serve your needs better than the one I suggest.

However, all business plans have the same basic shape. First, there is a section describing the concept of the organization, its history, and its mission. Second, a section describes in detail the customers or clients (the market) the organization seeks to serve. Third, there is an analysis of the competition or the competitive environment. Fourth, a section explains how the organization will use its resources (people and financial) to successfully attain its mission. Fifth (and finally), there is always a section that presents the financial implications of the organization's actions, both present and proposed. This financial model of the organization is at once the simplest part of the plan and the most dreaded.

Don't be fooled. The hard work of defining the concept, the customers, and the competition precedes the modeling of the organization in cash terms. Financial models rest on the many assumptions and collected information that go into the sections covering concept, customers, and competition. The numbers merely reflect those factors in a form that can be compared with the numbers for other similar organizations.

You may already have generated much of the content for your annual business plan: every time you apply for a major grant you have to provide it. The structure of a business plan is a little different and may encompass some areas that are unfamiliar to you.

Your strategic plan generated specific objectives, challenges, and opportunities that you will incorporate in your business plan.

The annual business plan may have a number of shapes. The one below is adapted from the *Business Planning Guide*, 9th edition (Kaplan Business, 2002). Feel free to adapt it to your own needs. One size does not fit all.

Cover Sheet
Executive Summary
Table of Contents
Statement of Purpose
Section One: The Organization
  A. Description of the Organization
  B. Services, Programs, and Products
  C. Marketing Plan
  D. Risks and Opportunities
      Barriers to Achieving Strategic Goals (optional)
      Operations Plan (optional)
  E. Management
  F. Personnel

G. Collaborating Agencies

Section Two: Financial Data
  A. Capital Equipment List (Current)
  B. Capital Equipment List (Anticipated)
  C. Balance Sheet
     Unit-Cost Analysis (optional)
  D. Revenue Projections
  E. Statement of Activities or P&L
  F. Cash Flow Projection or Cash Budget
  G. Three-Year P&L Projection
  H. Deviation Analysis

Section Three: Supporting Documents

*Sources:* any documents that you feel add weight or substance to your business plan. Examples include promotional materials, copies of important contracts, leases, and detailed resumes of principals.

# Explanation of Business Plan Format

## Beginning

### Cover Sheet

The cover sheet provides the name and address of the organization and its principals.

### Executive Summary

This can range from a short statement of intention that grabs the reader's attention ("elevator speech" or 30-second appeal) to a fuller description of what the organization is about and why it deserves funding.

The Executive Summary presents the highlights of the plan and states clearly what the plan is trying to accomplish, for example to raise funds for an endowment, to describe the organization to potential friends and allies, or to help better manage the nonprofit. Since nonprofits have two bottom lines, that is, a social mission as well as a financial mission (to start or grow the organization and to keep it solvent), a nonprofit executive summary tends to have two parts.

### Table of Contents

The Table of Contents may seem superfluous in a document that is only 20 or so pages long, but it helps the reader find the part that is most interesting to him or her. Think of it as a necessary courtesy.

### Statement of Purpose

This is where you put the mission statement and (if you wish) values and vision statements.

>**Mission Statement.** The mission statement is a concise statement of what your organization is trying to accomplish. This has been discussed in earlier chapters and polished in Chapter 7.

>**Statement of Purpose and Vision.** What will the world be like if you achieve your purpose? What is your vision? This section is not strictly necessary, but it is emotionally compelling and it can help you present your nonprofit in the most favorable light.

>**Values Statement.** Most values statements are meaningless: "We value honesty, goodness, loyalty, and compassion; we treat all staff with respect, etc., etc." It is optional.

## Section One: Information About the Organization

If your organization has applied for grants, you will be able to extract much of the material from grant proposals. More comes directly from the strategic plan you roughed out in Chapter 7.

### A. Description of the Organization

What is its history? Who founded it, when, where, and why? Is it a 501(c)(3)? Where is it located? What services are provided and to whom? This is where you expound on the concept and customer portion of the plan. This should be well-traveled territory.

### B. Services, Programs, and Products

What are the deliverables of the nonprofit? Describe (briefly) the services and programs offered. If you provide products, what are they?

### C. Marketing Plan

*Competition*

Who can or might provide the same services to the same clients? These are the direct competitors. You can learn from them: What are they doing right or wrong? How do they market their organizations to the public? Do you share stakeholders? And then there are the indirect competitors for the foundation dollars and other sources of funding. How about competition for staff, managers, and board members? For volunteers? If you aren't aware of what your competitors are doing, you stand to receive unpleasant surprises.

*Promotion, Advertising, and PR*

### D. Risks and Opportunities

The internal strengths and weakness of the organization are a proper part of the plan. What do you have to change? What can you build on? Funders are interested in this as a reality check. No nonprofit is without weakness and strengths, but you must know what they are in order to do something about them. The same thinking applies to external opportunities and threats. Left unnoticed, they hinder your organization's growth and may even endanger its survival. This is a reality check: it's not perfect, but it's a lot better than nothing. These risks and opportunities come from the strategic plan in Chapter 7.

**Barriers to Achieving Strategic Goals (Optional).** One common way to present this information is a table entitled "Barriers to Achieving Strategic Goals." In this you state the goals and note the problems with attaining them. You alert the reader that you have thought through the difficulties that lie ahead and have a plan to deal with them. These goals come straight from Chapter 7. You don't need to go into elaborate explanations of the goals; just note what they are and that they are backed up by your strategic plan. This is immensely reassuring to donors.

These problems may be hard to define, but it is important that you try. Are there economic changes? What about the impact of changing political forces? Think of the impact that 9/11 had on charitable giving. Think of the impact of Hurricane Katrina and surging energy costs.

Your goals and the action steps to meet your strategic goals come from Figure 7-7 in your strategic plan. The reason that you limited the number of strategic goals to no more than four is that you can't focus on more than a handful—and those must be the most important.

**Operations Plan (Optional).** There is some argument as to what an operations plan is and whether it should be part of the business plan. Some say it should be a separate document. Others think it is an extension of the action steps to meet strategic goals. Still others say it is somewhere in between, more formal than a simple listing of action steps and less comprehensive than a monthly to-do list.

The operations plan reveals how the services will be delivered, who is responsible for what, and how the operations can be fine-tuned. Use your judgment. A brand new organization won't need an operations plan until the initial activities show some results. A mature organization would be apt to use a separate, comprehensive operations plan, often in the form of an operating manual.

### E. Management

Initially this will consist of the Executive Committee and the executive director. As the nonprofit becomes bigger, the rule of thumb is that no more than five people should report directly to the executive director or to any other individual without very good reasons. Put the resumes of key personnel, board members, and staff in the appendix.

One very important part of the description of management is a succession plan. This should be formal if you have a clear successor for the executive director, but at the very least you should have a plan for filling the duties if, God forbid, the executive director were to be run down by a bus. The continuity of the nonprofit is a big concern to funders, and provisions for replacing key employees has to be addressed.

### F. Personnel

If your nonprofit has employees, what do they do? You don't have to go into detail, but it helps funders to know that your staff is competent. It's even more important that funders learn that you don't hire staff lightly or without careful thought. As a side note, what do you pay them? Is it in line with other nonprofits? You can get this information (at least salary ranges and in many cases job descriptions) from your local United Way.

### G. Collaborating Agencies

This list will coincide to some degree with competitors. What agencies can you work with to achieve your mission? Which agencies might be allies in the future? The nonprofit world turns on personal relationships, so you may want to seek out opportunities to work with others. Sitting on a potential ally's board is one way to do this.

### Summary

This should be just that, a summary narrative of the first section. This will be longer than the Executive Summary, but much shorter than even a condensed version of the first section.

In some ways it is a checklist. Have you covered mission? Check. Market? Check. Competition? Management? Strategies? Check. Some readers will turn to this right after the Executive Summary or after leafing through the financials.

## Section Two: Financial Information

This is where you quantify, in dollars, the costs (initial and ongoing) of running the nonprofit. It has two major sections: the balance sheet and the more dynamic cash flow and income and expense statements. See Chapter 8 for detailed explanations of these.

**A. Capital Equipment List (Current)**

**B. Capital Equipment List (Anticipated)**

**C. Balance Sheet or Statement of Financial Position**

This is a snapshot of the finances of the organization at a given time. It differs from the balance sheet of a for-profit organization in one important aspect: funds are divided into "unrestricted" and "restricted" categories.

**Unit-Cost Analysis.** What does it cost you to provide one unit of service? One visit to a client, one class, one counseling session, or whatever? When you factor in overhead costs (general and administrative costs), you may find that you are losing money you can ill afford on some services. If you make a conscious decision to keep providing those services, fine. But if you are blithely incurring hidden costs, you are heading for trouble. At the very least, whether you are a board member or the executive director, get expert financial advice on how to figure unit costs—and also how to create cash flow budgets, which are closely related to unit-cost analysis.

**D. Revenue Projections**

In the most general sense, what revenues can you assume for the coming year from fees, grants, donations, and fundraising events? This is as tricky for a new nonprofit as for any start-up, but it can be done. Experience will make the next projection more accurate, but you have to start somewhere.

Revenues are somewhat predictable, even early on. Will you have members who pay dues? Will clients pay a fee for service? Will you have a captive business that provides revenues (for example, short-term day care for people who are not clients)?

**E. Statement of Activities or P&L (Income Statement)**

Income is a measure of what comes in over a given period, usually a year (broken down by month). Whether the income comes in on schedule or not doesn't matter. Some expenses will be spread over the year (rent, insurance premiums, salaries), while others will be more time-specific. Don't worry yet. Think of a profit and loss statement in business. The P&L measures whether you have made a profit (or suffered a loss) during a stated period.

**F. Cash Flow Projection or Cash Budget**

Cash comes in from a very limited number of sources and goes out through many channels. Keeping the inflow and outflow balanced is at the heart of financial management. You have to keep track of how much comes in or goes out and when. Think of your personal checkbook. The aim of cash flow management is to always be liquid: you might have to borrow or postpone paying a bill, but bouncing checks is not a good option.

All things being equal, a cash flow budget is a better (that is, more useful) budget than an income and expense budget (P&L projection), but both aim at the same thing: having enough cash to keep up with the bills.

### G. Three-Year P&L Projection

This is less time sensitive than cash flow and indeed measures something different. Also known as an income and expense budget, the three-year (by month) P&L provides a look toward what you expect the organization will do in the near future. Longer scenarios are useless for small nonprofits.

### H. Deviation Analysis

Deviation analysis and other financial analyses put the budget to work. Basically, a deviation analysis checks actual performance against the budget each month, providing a quick check on how things are going.

## Section Three: Supporting Documents

These are extra goodies that have no obvious place in the business plan proper. They may include copies of leases and other important legal documents, descriptions of facilities, pictures and sketches of clients, resumes of key personnel and board members, encomiums and awards received by the organization and staff, examples of promotional materials, and more. Sometimes the added material makes a difference.

HELP
HERE

# Chapter 9

# Raising Money

**C**ASH, AS THEY SAY, IS KING. WITHOUT IT YOU CAN'T PROVIDE THE programs and services that your nonprofit is designed to provide. Unlike a for-profit business, you can't promise investors a return on their investment (except a psychic return) or look to future sales to provide a profit. So where do you get the necessary cash?

You ask for it. You ask individuals for direct donations. You ask foundations and government agencies and corporations for grants to support specific programs and projects. In time you can ask for direct donations from corporate and private philanthropies. The overall term for this asking is *fundraising*.

There are two fundraising commandments: *simplify* and *focus*. Many small nonprofits have trouble raising money because they pursue every conceivable opportunity, thereby diluting their efforts and losing sight of their mission.

Fundraising involves all acts of soliciting donations for a nonprofit agency. It includes efforts to raise money from:

▸ Individuals

▸ Grants

▸ Philanthropies (either private or corporate)

Add fees for service and similar revenues to the list. While these are not charitable donations, they can be a significant source of funds for a new nonprofit.

Most start-up nonprofits are limited to seeking donations from individuals and special events. (A very few might be able to secure government funding for a specific program, but this is rare.) Once up and running they might qualify for specific grants (usually program-related) and philanthropic donations. Program officers (who make the donation decisions in these organizations) look for a good track record, proven success, and a strong executive director as proof that their donations will make a positive difference and achieve their program and philanthropic goals. By definition, start-ups lack the first two and won't be able to overcome this barrier without an exceptionally well qualified and well connected ED.

*Most start-up nonprofits are limited to seeking donations from individuals and special events.*

In any case, fundraising starts simply enough.

## Kinds of Gifts

1. Annual giving to cover operations (unrestricted)
2. Mass mailings or phonathons to cover operations (unrestricted)
3. Program and project grants (restricted)
4. Fundraising events
5. Capital funds
6. In-kind contributions

It all begins with the case statement, a short (one or two pages) written statement that lets prospects know what you intend to do with their donations and why their donations will make a positive difference to the community. The case statement makes the case for making the donation, provides the basis for collateral material (brochures, letters, pamphlets, and so on), and helps keep the message of your nonprofit consistent and compelling. Without a clear case statement, your message will be muddled and lost.

# Step 1: The Case Statement

Here are some of the questions to answer in your case statement:

▶ Why are you in business? That is, what is the problem you are trying to alleviate or resolve? This is an expansion of your mission statement.

▶ What outcomes do you anticipate? These should be measurable and publicly observable, not a vague "improve lives" kind of statement. What specifically are you trying to accomplish with this specific program or service?

▶ How is your organization different from other organizations?

▶ How will you achieve your program and service goals? What methods will you use? Your coverage of this point doesn't have to be exhaustive.

▶ What major accomplishments has your nonprofit achieved? People give to successful organizations and tend to avoid giving to struggling ones.

▶ What is the history of the organization? When was it founded, by whom? How is it financed? What is the organization's philosophy? How does it work with other nonprofits?

*The overriding purpose of the case statement is to persuade the potential donor to open his or her checkbook and make a donation to your nonprofit.*

Notice that almost all of this information has been gathered in earlier chapters. It is longer than an elevator speech (that 30-second spiel designed to stimulate interest) but much shorter than a business or strategic plan. The overriding purpose of the case statement is to persuade the potential donor to open his or her checkbook and make a donation to your nonprofit.

To make it more effective, personalize the case statement. Sometimes this is called  seeking a "poster child" for the organization. The giving decision is ultimately based on emotion, not on pure reason alone. Accordingly, you want to put a face on the organization's beneficiaries. An after-school program will help a young woman avoid trouble, a dental program will help children have healthy teeth and gums, a homeless shelter will keep families out of the rain and cold. And so forth. Paint a picture with realistic people (or animals) receiving important benefits. That makes the case personal, as opposed to impersonal. It also makes it more exciting.

Who writes the case statement? Ideally, your stakeholders will all play a role. To save time and concentrate efforts, start with the board members and the executive director, who will be the primary askers. Sketch out a rough case statement and then ask for constructive criticism from other stakeholders, including employees, clients, early donors, and friends. Each group will have valuable suggestions. Ask for ideas on a poster child—and keep in mind that in advertising agencies the first few ideas are tossed out on the theory that early ideas are generally weak. If they indeed have value, that is, if they communicate the spirit and urgency of the program or service, those ideas will resurface.

Another dimension of revising the case statement involves aiming at your target. You will naturally slant the statement toward the people you are wooing. This does not mean that the case statement is entirely plastic: most of it will be constant. You will just emphasize facts and numbers to the analytically inclined, the emotional tugs to the sensitive, the prestige of donating to those who need reassurance that they will be joining a select group. This is not cynical, by the way. It is just smart selling.

# Step 2: Target Marketing

Target marketing, thoughtfully identifying the most likely potential donors, is one of the keys to successful fundraising. What is target marketing? Think of a target. At its center is a bull's-eye, surrounded by concentric bands that are successively further from the center. You aim for the center, the bull's-eye, where you gain the most points. If you are a bit off, you hit the first ring, which will give you fewer points.

Now think of your limited marketing dollars as a quiver of arrows. All fundraising has monetary costs. How can you maximize the return on your investment? Simple: aim carefully. Go for the biggest payoff, the bull's-eye. With practice you'll improve your aim.

Start with your board and their contacts. These usually will include the earliest donors and people like them. Following well-proven marketing techniques, your chances of successful fundraising starts with people who have already given to your organization, followed closely by those who have already donated to a similar cause. You want to grow the bull's-eye by turning people from potential donors to actual donors. Or, put another way, you want to foster a relationship with more and more individuals. Your staff, friends, and other stakeholders will help you identify more potential donors. Ask for referrals (this is what all salespeople do) and follow up. Slowly, step by step, this will yield a stable base of donors. And, if you are smart, you can begin to cultivate those donors who can make major contributions.

The same process applies when seeking funds from corporations, philanthropies, and/or government agencies. You look for the early donors and cultivate them; then you look for more people like them and repeat the process. An important corollary: corporations, philanthropies, and government agencies don't make the decision to give money. It's individuals in those organizations who make the decisions, and you have to carefully nurture your relationship with those individuals. In a very real sense, all giving is individual.

*Think of your limited marketing dollars as a quiver of arrows. All fundraising has monetary costs. How can you maximize the return on your investment? Simple: aim carefully.*

# Step 3: Start with Individual Solicitations

Getting funds for a new nonprofit is very similar to getting funds for a new for-profit venture. Traditionally you begin by investing your own assets. Then you turn to the three Fs: *family*, *friends*, and *fools*.

Family and friends have an obvious, natural reason to invest in your new venture. If your idea is as good as you think it is, then you are doing your family and friends a favor by allowing them to invest in your start-up.

Fools are persons who think you have a good business idea with a real shot at success. The label of "fools" may sound harsh, but the success rate of new ventures, relative to other, less risky investments, is dismal.

Take the same approach with your nonprofit. First, if you're not willing to invest in your nonprofit, why should anybody else? Second, if the case for the nonprofit is compelling to you, it probably will also be appealing to your family and friends. The third group of start-up nonprofit investors might be *fanatics* (not fools) who see the same social benefit that drives your ideas.

What you cannot do is hope to attract bank funds (banks have a role to play later, once you have a track record) or philanthropic and grant funds. These organizations aren't interested in start-ups.

## Customers vs. Clients

Customers are people who write you checks. Clients are people to whom you provide services and programs; they may or may not also be customers. Keep these two concepts distinct.

Part of your job as a fundraiser is to identify those persons and organizations likely to be interested in the programs and services that you offer. Asking people for a donation to a nonprofit that has no interest to them is folly. Targeting a small number of potential donors is an efficient way to focus your efforts.

## Personalized Appeals to Core Supporters

Make personalized appeals to your core supporters. The most efficient method of reaching your core supporters is by visiting them individually. You may do this alone or, more commonly, a board member and the executive director may make the visit.

Before you go, rehearse what you plan to do. What will you say? How large a contribution will you solicit? What kind of supporting material will you take along?

The beauty of a personal visit is that you will be forming a relationship with the individual. You can tailor your presentation based on his or her response. Ask for referrals. Ask for a critique of your solicitation. You are speaking to persons who have already made a commitment to your nonprofit, so asking them for money is not an imposition. While you might feel awkward the first few times you go out to raise funds on a personal basis, that feeling will soon wear off and you may even find that you enjoy the process.

Why rehearse? Simple: winging it won't work for most of us. By having a script that you can fall back on, including an ask level, you develop a consistent approach that you can improve. One suggestion is to make a list of the 100 (or 50 or 25) persons you target for an individual visit and then roughly rank them in terms of their potential value to your organization. Some ranking criteria: potential donation, strength as a referral source, position in community, political or other position. Then visit the list in reverse order, starting with people you rank lowest. The idea is that by the time you get partway through the list you will have honed your presentations and learned the major objections and how to deal with them and you will know what works best. That will concentrate your best efforts on the best prospects.

Individual personalized visiting is a great source of unrestricted funds to cover the unglamorous but vital overhead expenses. It is also (see below) a way to pave the way for planned giving and other capital raising efforts.

Make sure to ask—and ask again. A visit without an ask is a waste of everybody's time.

*Individual personalized visiting is a great source of unrestricted funds to cover the unglamorous but vital overhead expenses.*

## Annual Fund Appeals

Most nonprofits conduct annual fund appeals in which they invite their stakeholders and other potential supporters to each make a small donation to cover the expenses of running the organization. These are appeals for unrestricted funds.

Most appeals rely on mail to deliver a series of requests for money. One or two letters won't break through the clutter of mail the recipients are receiving. Some experts call for as many as eight or even more mailings. The incremental costs (using a mass mailing permit) are small for each additional mailing.

The key here is to have a clean mailing list. Do not purchase or rent a mailing list unless you have money to burn. Instead, compile your own list, starting once more with current and past supporters and stakeholders, paying particular emphasis to those persons who have benefited from your programs and services. A compiled list is built around people who have expressed an interest in what you are trying to accomplish. These are selected people, already qualified.

Phonathons are another way to conduct an annual appeal. The same list qualifications apply: make sure the people on the list are involved in some way with your organization. "Blind" calls are seldom productive for nonprofits and may indeed stir up resentment.

If you decide on a phonathon, prepare a script for every caller to follow. This facilitates data collection and will help your organization improve results in the future. Hire a professional to prepare the script. The difference between the results of a good professional script and the results of an amateur effort will astound you. In most cases a good script will pay for itself.

E-mail is an increasingly popular fundraising method. Once again, the results depend on the quality of the list. Advantages of e-mail include cost (very low), information transfer (very high if properly prepared), ease of collecting information (high), and flexibility. You can make changes very easily.

*If you can, sample a small number of prospects before rolling out a full mailing, phone calling, or e-mailing.*

If you can, sample a small number of prospects before rolling out a full mailing, phone calling, or e-mailing. These forms of direct mass marketing have a logic all of their own, and small changes can lead to big differences in results. Accordingly, most nonprofits try to get direct marketing expertise on their boards or, failing that, rely on outside advisors to help develop the mailing package (cover letter, pamphlet or collateral, response device), the script and record, the e-mail, or the Web site. This is too important to be left to learn-it-yourself efforts.

## A Note on Timing

Timing your annual appeal can be tricky. Check with the United Way (if you have one and hope to secure grants from them) to make sure you don't violate their time-out period. Other commonsense rules apply. When is it convenient for people in your target market to make donations? For some it will be the end of their tax year, for others the end of the calendar year. The better you know your target market, the better you can make this kind of judgment.

## Special Events and Benefits

Even a prospective nonprofit can run a successful fundraising event. It might be a cocktail party, a tea, a golf tournament, a famous speaker, a dinner dance, an auction, a day out on a yacht.... The possibilities are almost endless.

As with any fundraising effort, start with a goal in mind. How much cash do you hope to gain (net of expenses)? How many people must you attract to have a shot at reaching that goal? If holding a successful special event were easy, there would be many more of them. Unfortunately, there are plenty of fundraising events that don't come close to meeting expenses.

Marketing is as important as raising money. Think about it. Most benefits have two goals: raising awareness of the nonprofit's mission and raising money. In some cases raising money is considered secondary, especially if the nonprofit is new and unfamiliar. A successful event will elevate awareness of the organization.

How do you plan for a successful event? Start with the goal: unrestricted cash and/or marketing goals. Then ask these questions:

▶ Are there timing issues? Well-established conflicting events can be a damper on your efforts. At times there seem to be golf tournaments or auctions every day.

▶ Who will be on the guest list? Think *target marketing*. You will want to invite your core supporters, your stakeholders, potential donors, and perhaps some community leaders. The event must be tailored to their schedules and desires—and if you try to reach too many people, you almost guarantee failure. Keep it simple.

▶ What will you ask for? Donations, true. But other asks are important: recruiting new board members, advisory board members, referrals. Simply getting to know more people is valuable; the more friends you can make for your nonprofit, the better.

▶ Should there be an entry fee? That depends on the event and the crowd. This is a judgment call. If you do ask for a donation, think carefully about how much (or little) to ask. If your audience is well-heeled, ask high. If not, ask low or don't ask at all.

▶ What is the budget for the event? A budget is vital: expenses can easily get out of control. The budgeted costs will affect what you ask for. Plan ahead on the financial front and prevent unnecessary losses.

▶ Can you solicit in-kind gifts? Perhaps a caterer will provide services at cost or a facility will waive charges. You have to ask for this kind of donation; if you do not ask, you will not receive.

## Memberships

Memberships provide another source of unrestricted funds. Many well-known nonprofits are purely memberships: Lions, Kiwanis, Rotary, and so on. Some religious groups are quasi-membership organizations. Some nonprofits are barred from offering memberships due to the terms of their major funders, while others find that the added burden of keeping members happy is not worth the effort. However, if your nonprofit can easily provide basic membership benefits (newsletters, lowered fees for events, preferred treatment of some kind), it's worth considering, since membership income tends to be very stable over time.

## Planned Giving

*Planned giving is a long-term effort that begins with establishing and nurturing a relationship with the prospective giver.*

Especially helpful for capital funds and endowments, planned giving is a long-term effort that begins with establishing and nurturing a relationship with the prospective giver. Methods can range from providing financial planning services (use a professional) to a group, encouraging inclusion of the nonprofit in wills, and using life insurance or greatly appreciated stock to fund a major gift (with consequent tax savings) to more sophisticated methods that are beyond the scope of all but the largest nonprofits. As always, the better you know the prospects, the greater the chances of success.

# Step 4: Foundations and Other Funding Sources

There are over 30,000 charitable foundations. They represent a rich source of funds for nonprofits—usually for restricted funds for specific programs or services, less often for unrestricted operating funds.

How do you get funded by one of these? The same way as you get funding from individuals. You have to know what you are seeking, do research on foundations that might be interested in what you are doing, and establish a relationship with people in those organizations who make funding

### Five Sources of Funds

▶ Individuals
▶ Government
▶ Business
▶ Foundations
▶ Nonprofit Organizations

decisions (remember that organizations don't make decisions, people do). Then and only then can you sensibly ask for funds.

Foundations, whether public or private, are very explicit in their interests. You can research them via the Internet, go to the library, or (more efficient) ask your peers and the helpful people at the United Way for guidance.

Local charitable foundations serve local nonprofit needs. Community foundations are very approachable and are a major source of funds for capacity building, which is jargon for helping small nonprofits acquire skills (planning, grant writing, negotiating, board training, and so on). If your nonprofit would benefit from a strategic planning retreat, for example, your community foundation (or other local foundation) might be willing to pay for a facilitator to help with the strategic planning process. Make the relationship, get clear on your needs, and ask for their assistance. Even if they say no, they will go out of their way to explain why, how you can improve your chances, and let you in on their grant cycles (timing is important) and decision criteria.

The big independent foundations (Ford, Gates, Rockefeller, and so on) are not likely to give money to small nonprofits. Unless you have a really big idea that fits their stated criteria, don't bother—and even if you do, the chances are slim.

Corporations and other businesses have charitable wings, usually under the aegis of community or public relations. Some are targeted frequently: banks, financial service companies, law firms, utilities, and medical businesses are besieged by requests. Ask them what their donation criteria are. If you fit them, great, but if you do not, don't waste your time or theirs. What they may be willing to provide even to a brand new nonprofit is used furniture and equipment. They also are a great source of board members. Some companies even require junior officers to be active in local nonprofits as part of their training.

The United Way and other federated fund drives operate on a local level. They are major trainers for nonprofit boards and staff as well as substantial funders. However, in recent years their trend has been to concentrate on a few broad areas (medical and dental, homelessness, and early childhood education are favorite areas of interest), so they are less apt to provide direct funding. Ask them. You have to get to know them very well, because they act as a clearinghouse for nonprofit information and referral.

Service clubs such as Rotary, Elks, Lions, and many others have a strong local presence. They have been known to adopt small nonprofits, steering funds and raising awareness as part of their service duties. They also provide

*Community foundations are very approachable and are a major source of funds for capacity building, which is jargon for helping small nonprofits acquire skills.*

a great venue to speak, allowing you to reach business and community leaders in a favorable environment. Chambers of Commerce provide great speaking venues, though not a funding source.

Public funding sources include federal, state, and local agencies. The good thing is that they provide a lot of money. The bad thing is that even if you are able to secure a grant, a contract, or a direct-purchase/fee-for-service deal with a government agency, the paperwork and the oversight can be very burdensome. (Fair enough; it's public money.)

# Step 5: Getting Grants

Unless you have grant-writing experience, hire a pro to help out. You can learn by doing, to be sure, but it will take far longer than you can probably afford. There are literally thousands of books on grant writing, but working with a pro will speed you up the learning curve, give you insights into the process from both the grantor and the grantee sides, and markedly increase your chances of getting funded.

You should also look for local grant-writing seminars. This is a strong point of your local United Way—the staff benefits by eventually receiving well-thought-out grant proposals and saves time by helping nonprofits learn not to submit long-shot proposals.

Start by deciding which funding sources to target. A minimal requirement is a close fit between your needs and their interests. Sometimes foundations issue requests for proposals (RFPs), stating their interest in funding some specific area of interest. You propose (following their guidelines, which they will provide) and they dispose.

There is a danger: twisting your mission to fit their requirements on the theory that some money, any money, will be helpful and, after all, it's pretty close to your mission…. Beware of *mission creep*. It is insidious. While you might get some funds, in the long run it will cost your nonprofit credibility.

Return to your case statement. Slant it to the selected funder's requirements. Good grant writers can do this in their sleep.

Document the need for the services and programs you provide. Make it clear that you will avoid duplicating the efforts of other nonprofits in the area.

Get to know the funders. They will work with you. You want to establish a long-term relationship with both individuals and the foundation itself; this is a relationship that must be nourished.

Remember that the foundations make a point of being clear in their directions to potential recipients of their funds. Your hardest job is making sure that you follow their instructions. Once again, make it easy on yourself by working with a professional grant writer until you feel confident in your ability to successfully apply for grant monies.

# Chapter 10

# Resources

**B**EWARE OF INFORMATION OVERLOAD, ESPECIALLY IF STARTING AND managing a nonprofit is new to you. You can easily find thousands of Web sites, hundreds of books and magazines, and organizations set up to help nonprofits. Keep it as simple as possible.

## Organizations

Your best resource is your state's center for nonprofits, if it has one. (Centers are listed by state at the end of this chapter.) These centers generally provide training, forums to meet with your peers, links to in-state sources of assistance, and much more. They generally have libraries focused on nonprofit management, a shortcut to finding the right books and publications for you and your organization.

On a local level, check your United Way or similar community organization. Those people have a strong interest in helping you do a better job. In particular, they are interested in building capacity in small nonprofits. Their training in developing objective and measurable outcomes is outstanding. Strong measurable outcomes are a key to gaining funding from established philanthropies and serious donors. The United Way also provides lists of qualified local consultants with specialized skills.

Most colleges and universities have extension courses to help nonprofit managers sharpen their skills. Check them out. Basic management skills can be learned—thousands of people have picked up financial, marketing, and personnel management skills from these programs. The beauty of extension courses is their flexibility. Look for evening and weekend courses. Some offer distant learning programs online that you can take at your convenience.

If you are fortunate, you may have a local charitable foundation (such as the Greater Piscataqua Community Foundation) that will help you learn the ins and outs of fundraising, provide modest financial assistance to build capacity, link you with other nonprofit executives, and provide a variety of trainings. Even if you are not seeking funding, such organizations provide valuable services. Ask them.

# Books

This is a highly subjective list. Amazon.com lists some 46,000 books on non-profits, a daunting challenge. As mentioned earlier, your local librarian should be able to help you find the most appropriate books and other publications.

*Starting and Running a Nonprofit Organization*, 2nd edition. Joan M. Hummel. Revised by the Center for Nonprofit Management, Graduate School of Business, University of St. Thomas. © 1980, 1996 University of Minnesota Press, Minneapolis MN. This is an excellent how-to guide with good forms and charts.

*Nonprofit Kit for Dummies,* 2nd edition. Stan Hutton and Frances Phillips. © 2001, 2005 John Wiley & Sons, Indianapolis IN. This book is voluminous and thorough. Some beginners are overwhelmed by this amount of information, but it is an excellent resource. It contains a CD with many forms and references.

*Managing a Nonprofit Organization in the Twenty-First Century.* Thomas Wolf. © 1999 Simon & Schuster, New York NY. This book is very strong on managing people as well as handling the finances. It provides good checklists.

*Governing Boards*, 2nd edition. Cyril O. Houle. © 1989, 1997 Jossey-Bass, San Francisco CA. This is the definitive book on board duties and composition, from the premier publisher of nonprofit books. Go to www.josseybass.com/WileyCDA/ to view its other books in the nonprofit category.

*Outcomes Measurement in the Human Services: Cross-Cutting Issues and Methods.* Edward J. Mullen and Jennifer L. Magnabosco, editors. © 1997 NASW Press, Washington DC. This text is fairly heavy going, but if you are concerned with setting useful outcomes, it is useful.

*The Cash Flow Management Book for Nonprofits.* Murray Dropkin and Allyson Hayden. © 2001 John Wiley & Sons, New York NY. Subtitled *A Step-by-Step Guide for Managers, Consultants, and Boards,*" this is another fine Jossey-Bass book, a how-to guide to managing a nonprofit's finances.

*Financial Management for Nonprofits: The Complete Guide to Maximizing Resources and Managing Assets.* Jae K. Shim and Joel G. Siegel. ©1997 McGraw-Hill, New York NY. This book is not for the beginner, but great for the more experienced financial manager.

*Wiley Not-for-Profit Accounting Field Guide, 2003.* Richard F. Larkin and Marie DiTommaso. © 1999, 2003 John Wiley & Sons, New York NY. This is advanced material for people more experienced in nonprofit finances. Your treasurer and accountant will find it helpful.

*Creating and Implementing Your Strategic Plan: A Workbook for Public and Nonprofit Organizations,* 2nd edition. John M. Bryson and Farnum K. Alston. © 1996, 2004 Jossey-Bass, San Francisco CA. A well thought-out workbook to guide you through a detailed strategic planning process.

*Strategic Planning for Nonprofit Organizations,* 2nd edition. Michael Allison and Jude Kaye. © 1997, 2005 CompassPoint Nonprofit Services, John Wiley & Sons, New York NY. This book is a step up from *Creating and Implementing Your Strategic Plan,* suitable for the more experienced nonprofit executive or consultant.

*The Board Member's Guide to Fund Raising.* Fisher Howe. © 1991 Jossey-Bass, San Francisco CA. This is the only book that addresses the role of board members in their arguably most important task: raising enough money so the nonprofit can achieve its goals. Although old, it is an invaluable resource, recommended for all board members.

*Fundraising for Dummies,* 2nd edition. John Mutz and Katherine Murray. © 2000, 2005 John Wiley & Sons, Indianapolis IN. A comprehensive resource for all nonprofits. You cannot know too much about fundraising and this is a fine resource.

*Nonprofit Personnel Policies*, 2nd edition. Jamie Whaley, editor. © 2001, Aspen Publishers, Gaithersburg MD. This is an excellent all-purpose personnel management book for nonprofit managers.

# Web Sites

These Web sites have been culled from a list of hundreds.

### Idealist.org (Action Without Borders)
*idealist.org*
This site offers has a lot of tools and information, simply presented. Check out The Nonprofit FAQ—"based on questions and answers about nonprofit organizations exchanged on the Internet since 1994"—it's very extensive. This is a great place to start.

### Free Management Library
*www.managementhelp.org*
This "Complete, highly integrated library for nonprofits and for-profits" is another general site with special focus on new nonprofits. It has a list of 675 books and articles indexed by 675 topics and continuously updated. There's also a Free Complete Toolkit for Boards—*www.managementhelp.org/boards/boards.htm*—that contains a wealth of information for board members and those who would evaluate board members and Human Resource Management Information for Nonprofit Organizations—*www.managementhelp.org/hr_mgmnt/np_spcf.htm*—that does the same for staff.

### Nonprofit Financial Center: Online Guides
*www.nfconline.org/main/info/guides.htm*
This Web site offers online guides to assessment tools, strategy, financial reporting, budget and cash flow, starting a nonprofit, accounting rules and regulations, human resources, organizational policies, audits, and bookkeeping systems and accounting software. If you need help with finances this is a good place to start.

### Financial Management for Nonprofits
*oncampus.richmond.edu/connect/nonprofit/finance/finance-index.html*
On this Web page, it states, "Many nonprofit organizations do not understand the opportunities that come from learning the pros and cons of various forms of financial management." This section of a series of pages for nonprofits provides "basic information to guide you to the best financial management for your organization and make the most of your financial systems."

**Nonprofit Financial Center: Financial Management Library**

*www.nfconline.org/main/info/library/library_17.htm*

This Web page shows another aspect of the NFC: it maintains a library of materials covering all facets of nonprofit financial management.

**New Hampshire Center for Nonprofits**

*www.nhnonprofits.org/newsite*

There are organizations in every state similar to the New Hampshire Center for Nonprofits. You may have to look for them, but they are the single best resource for learning about what other nonprofits are doing.

**Charity Channel**

*charitychannel.com*

The goal of the Charity Channel is "To create a place where nonprofit professionals can connect, learn from each other, share information and work together to advance the cause of philanthropy." It charges a modest subscriber fee for its varied services. Its We Review feature (*charitychannel.com/enewsletters/wr*) can help you keep current on books for nonprofits.

**Energize, Inc.**

*www.energizeinc.com*

This is a fine Web site aimed at managing volunteers, a vital topic for all nonprofits but especially small or new organizations. See its library and referral networks.

**Delaware Association of Nonprofit Agencies**

*www.delawarenonprofit.org/infocentral/boardmanage.php*

This site represents the kind of resource that exists in almost all states. It provides links to information and advice that can help nonprofit managers in any state.

# State Nonprofit Centers

**Alabama**

Nonprofit Resource Center of Alabama
3324 Independence Drive, Suite 100
Birmingham, AL 35209
Phone: (205) 879-4712, (888) 466-4777 (toll-free)
Fax: (205) 879-4724
E-mail: george@nrca.info
Web: www.nrca.info

**Alaska**

## Alaska Association of Nonprofit Corporations

Nancy K. Scheetz-Freymiller, President
420 Kayak Drive
Anchorage, AK 99515
Phone: (907) 345-6714
Fax: N/A
E-mail: nscheetz@gci.net
Web: N/A

## Foraker Group

880 H Street, Suite 100
Anchorage, AK 99501
Phone: (907) 743-1200, (877) 834-5003 (toll-free)
Fax: (907) 276-5014
E-mail: info@forakergroup.org
Web: www.forakergroup.org

**Arizona**

## Alliance of Arizona Nonprofits

P.O. Box 16162
Phoenix, AZ 85011-6162
Phone: N/A
Fax: N/A
E-mail: N/A
Web: www.arizonanonprofits.org

## Center for Nonprofit Leadership and Management

Arizona State University
Mail Code 4120
411 N. Central Avenue, Suite 500
Phoenix, AZ 85004-0691
Phone: (602) 496-0500
Fax: (602) 496-0952
E-mail: nonprofit@asu.edu
Web: www.asu.edu/copp/nonprofit

**Arkansas**

## Nonprofit Resources, Inc.

3805 W. 12th Street, Suite 104
Little Rock, AR 72204

Phone: (501) 379-1558
Fax: (501)-374-6548
E-mail: N/A
Web: nonprofitarkansas.dewdesigns.com/consul.htm

## California

**California Association of Nonprofits**
520 South Grand Avenue, Suite 695
Los Angeles, CA 90071
Phone: (213) 347-2070
Fax: (213) 347-2080
E-mail: info@canonprofits.org
Web: www.canonprofits.org

## Colorado

**Colorado Nonprofit Association**
455 Sherman Street, Suite 207
Denver, CO 80203-4494
Phone: (303) 832-5710, (800) 333-6554
Fax: N/A
E-mail: info@coloradononprofits.org
Web: www.coloradononprofits.org

**Center for Nonprofit Excellence**
518 North Nevada Avenue
Colorado Springs, CO 80903
Phone: (719) 575-4341
Fax: (719) 955-0765
E-mail: info@ppnp.org
Web: www.cnecoloradosprings.org

## Connecticut

**Connecticut Association of Nonprofits**
90 Brainard Road
Hartford, CT 06114
Phone: (860) 525-5080
Fax: (860) 525-5088
E-mail: info@ctnonprofits.org
Web: www.ctnonprofits.org

## Delaware

**Delaware Association of Nonprofit Agencies**
100 W. 10th Street, Suite 102
Wilmington, DE 19801
Phone: (302) 777-5500
Fax: (302) 777-5386
E-mail: dana@delawarenonprofit.org
Web: www.delawarenonprofit.org

## District of Columbia

**Center for Nonprofit Advancement**
1666 K Street, NW, Suite 440
Washington, DC 20006
Phone: (202) 457-0540
Fax: (202) 457-0549
E-mail: info@nonprofitadvancement.org
Web: www.nonprofitadvancement.org

## Florida

**Florida Association of Nonprofit Organizations**
7480 Fairway Drive, Suite 206
Miami Lakes, FL 33014
Phone: (305) 557-1764
Fax: (305) 821-5528
E-mail: fanoinfo@fano.org
Web: www.fano.org

**Nonprofit Center of Northeast Florida, Inc.**
1301 Riverplace Boulevard, Suite 301
Jacksonville, FL 32207
Phone: (904) 390-3222
Fax: (904) 390-7367
E-mail: rcoughlin@nonprofitjax.org
Web: www.nonprofitjax.org

## Georgia

**Georgia Center for Nonprofits**
50 Hurt Plaza, S.E., Suite 845
Atlanta, GA 30303
Phone: (678) 916-3000, (800) 959-5015
Fax: (404) 521-0487

E-mail: info@gcn.org.
Web: www.gcn.org

## Hawaii

### Hawai'i Alliance of Nonprofit Organizations
Hawaii Community Services Council
33 South King Street, Suite 501
Honolulu, HI 96813
Phone: (808) 529-0466
Fax: (808) 529-0477
E-mail: info@hcsc-hawaii.org
Web: www.hcsc-hawaii.org

## Idaho

### Idaho Nonprofit Development Center
Park Center Pointe
1509 Tyrell Lane, Suite A
Boise, ID 83706
Phone: (208) 424-2229
Fax: (208) 424-2294
E-mail: info@idahononprofits.org
Web: idahononprofits.org

## Illinois

### Illinois Association of Nonprofit Organizations
c/o Ellen Dick
Metro Management, Inc.
8 S. Michigan Avenue, Suite 3000
Chicago, Il 60603
Phone: (312) 236-9673, (708) 386-9385 (Fridays only)
Fax: (708) 386-0462
E-mail: N/A
Web: N/A

### Donors Forum of Chicago
208 South LaSalle, Suite 740
Chicago, IL 60604-1006
Phone: (312) 578-0090
Fax: (312) 578-0103
E-mail: info@donorsforum.org
Web: www.donorsforum.org

## Indiana

**Indiana Association of Nonprofit Organizations**
c/o The NonProfit Team, Inc.
1720 Market Tower
10 West Market Street
Indianapolis, IN 46204
Phone: (317) 464-5156
Fax: (317) 464-5146
E-mail: info@npteam.org
Web: www.npteam.org

## Iowa

**Iowa Nonprofit Resource Center**
130 Grand Avenue Court
Iowa City, IA 52242
Phone: (866) 500-8980 (toll-free), (319) 335-9765
Fax: (319) 335-7614
E-mail: law-nonprofit@uiowa.ed
Web: nonprofit.law.uiowa.edu

## Kansas

**Kansas Non Profit Association**
c/o Mainstream, Inc.
P.O. Box 47054
Topeka, KS 66647
Phone: (800) 582-1428, (785) 266-6422
Fax: (785) 266-2113
E-mail: knpa@mainstreaminc.net
Web: www.ksnonprofitassoc.net

## Kentucky

**Nonprofit Leadership Initiative**
University of Kentucky
500 Garrigus Building
Lexington, KY 40546-0215
Phone: (859) 257-2542
Fax: (859) 323-2715
E-mail: emailus@kynonprofits.org
Web: www.kynonprofits.org

**Louisiana**

**Louisiana Association of Nonprofit Organizations**
700 N. 10th Street, Suite 250
Baton Rouge, LA 70802
P.O. Box 3808
Baton Rouge, LA 70821-3808
Phone: (225) 343-5266
Fax: (225) 343-5363
E-mail: contactus@lano.org
Web: www.lano.org

**Maine**

**Maine Association of Nonprofits**
565 Congress Street, Suite 301
Portland, ME 04101
Phone: (207) 871-1885
Fax: (207) 780-0346
E-mail: technicalassistance@nonprofitmaine.org
Web: www.nonprofitmaine.org

**Maryland**

**Maryland Association of Nonprofit Organizations**
190 W. Ostend Street, Suite 201
Baltimore, MD 21230
Phone: (410) 727-6367, (800) 273-6367
Fax: (410) 727-1914, (877) 565-0942 (toll-free)
8720 Georgia Avenue, Suite 303
Silver Spring, MD 20910
Phone: (301) 565-0505, (877) 565-0707 (toll-free)
Fax: (301) 565-0606
E-mail: eknight@mdnonprofit.org
Web: www.marylandnonprofits.org

**Massachusetts**

**Massachusetts Council of Human Service Providers, Inc.**
250 Summer Street, Suite 237
Boston, MA 02210
Phone: (617) 428-3637
Fax: (617) 428-1533
E-mail: mripple@providers.org
Web: www.providers.org

## Michigan

**Michigan Nonprofit Association**
1048 Pierpont Drive, Suite 3
Lansing, MI 48911
Phone: (517) 492-2400, (888) 242-7075 (toll-free in MI)
Fax: (517) 492-2410
E-mail: mnaweb@action.mnaonline.org
Web: www.mnaonline.org

## Minnesota

**Minnesota Council of Nonprofits**
2314 University Avenue W. #20
St. Paul, MN 55114
Phone: (651) 642-1904, (800) 289-1904 (toll-free in MN)
Fax: (651) 642-1517
E-mail: info@mncn.org
Web: www.mncn.org

## Mississippi

**Mississippi Center for Nonprofits**
700 North Street, Suite 201
Jackson, MS 39202
Phone: (601) 968-0061
Fax: (601) 352-8820
E-mail: mcn@msnonprofits.org
Web: www.msnonprofits.org

## Missouri

**Council on Philanthropy**
4747 Troost Avenue, Suite 204
Kansas City, MO 64110
P.O. Box 5813
Kansas City, MO 64171
Phone: (816) 235-6259
Fax (816) 235-5727
E-mail council@kcphilnet.org
Web: www.kcphilnet.org

## Montana

**Montana Nonprofit Association**
432 Last Chance Gulch, Suite E
P.O. Box 1744

Helena, MT 59624
Phone: (406) 449-3717
Fax: (406) 449-3718
E-mail: info@mtnonprofit.org
Web: www.mtnonprofit.org

## Nebraska

**Nonprofit Association of the Midlands**
5002 South 24th Street, Suite 201
Omaha, NE 68107
Phone: (402) 557-5800
Fax: (402) 557-5803
E-mail: david@nonprofitam.org
Web: www.nonprofitam.org

## Nevada

**Nevada Association of Nonprofit Organizations**
3753 Howard Hughes Parkway, Suite 200
Las Vegas, NV 89109
Phone: (702) 784-7608, (888) 604-6273 (toll-free)
Fax: (702) 892-0655
E-mail: nano@nevadanonprofits.org
Web: www.nevadanonprofits.org

## New Hampshire

**New Hampshire Center for Nonprofits**
10 Ferry Street, #315
Concord, NH 03301
Phone: (603) 225-1947
Fax: 603) 228-5574
E-mail: info@nhnonprofits.org
Web: www.nhnonprofits.org

## New Jersey

**Center for Non-Profit Corporations**
1501 Livingston Avenue
North Brunswick, NJ 08902
Phone: (732) 227-0800
Fax: (732) 227-0087
E-mail: center@njnonprofits.org
Web: www.njnonprofits.org

**New Mexico**

NGO New Mexico: New Mexico's Association of Nonprofit Organizations
P.O. Box 5398
Santa Fe, NM 87502
Phone: (505) 820-7056
Fax: (505) 820-7055
E-mail: mmcinnes@ngonm.org
Web: ngonm.org

**New York**

Council of Community Services of New York State, Inc.
272 Broadway
Albany, NY 12204
Phone: (518) 434-9194, (800) 515-5012
Fax: (518) 434-0392
E-mail: info@ccsnys.org
Web: www.ccsnys.org

Nonprofit Coordinating Committee of New York, Inc.
1350 Broadway, No. 1801
New York, NY 10018
Phone: (212) 502-4191
Fax: (212) 502-4189
E-mail: info@npccny.org
Web: www.npccny.org

**North Carolina**

North Carolina Center for Nonprofits
1110 Navaho Drive, Suite 200
Raleigh, NC 27609-7322
Phone: (919) 790-1555
Fax: (919) 790-5307
E-mail: info@ncnonprofits.org
Web: www.ncnonprofits.org

**North Dakota**

North Dakota Association of Nonprofit Organizations
P.O. Box 1091
1605 E. Capitol Avenue
Bismarck, ND 58502
Phone: (701) 258-9101, (888) 396-3266 (toll-free)

Fax: N/A
E-mail: ndano@btinet.net
Web: www.ndano.org

**Ohio**

**Ohio Association of Nonprofit Organizations**
100 E. Broad Street, Suite 2440
Columbus, OH 43215-3119
Phone: (614) 280-0233
Fax: (614) 280-0657
E-mail: info@oano.org
Web: www.ohiononprofits.org

**Oklahoma**

**Oklahoma Center for Nonprofits**
923 N. Robinson, Suite 400
Oklahoma City, OK 73102-2203
Phone: (405) 236-8133
Fax: (405) 272-0436
110 West 7th, Suite 2611
Tulsa, OK 74119-1031
Phone: (918) 579-1900
Fax: (918) 579-5176
E-mail: info@oklahomacenterfornonprofits.org
Web: www.oklahomacenterfornonprofits.org

**Oklahoma Community Institute**
900 N. Stiles
P.O. Box 1113
Oklahoma City, OK 73101-1113
Phone: (405) 815-5191
Fax: (405) 815-5193
E-mail: okcom@ocionline.org
Web: www.ocionline.org

**Oregon**

**Technical Assistance for Community Services**
1001 SE Water Avenue, Suite 490
Portland, OR 97214
Phone: (503) 239-4001
Fax: (503) 236-8313

E-mail: info@tacs.org
Web: www.tacs.org

**Oregon Nonprofit Association**
c/o Oregon Involved
1001 SE Water Avenue, Suite 490
Portland, OR 97214
Phone: (503) 239-4001
Fax: (503) 236-8313
E-mail: info@oregoninvolved.org
Web: www.oregoninvolved.org

## Pennsylvania

**Pennsylvania Association of Nonprofit Organizations**
777 East Park Drive, Suite 300
Harrisburg, PA 17111
Phone: (717) 236-8584
Fax: (717) 236-8767
E-mail: jenn@pano.org
Web: www.pano.org

## Rhode Island

**The Rhode Island Foundation**
1 Union Station
Providence, RI 02903
Phone: (401) 274-4564
Fax: (401) 331-8085
E-mail: cperry@rifoundation.org
Web: www.rifoundation.org

**Executive Service Corps of New England in Rhode Island**
Jeanne Waldinger, Vice President of Consulting Services
P.O. Box 5428
Wakefield, RI 02880
Phone: (401) 783-3141
Fax: (401) 783-0541
E-mail: jwaldinger@escne.org
Web: escne.org/Rhode_Island/rhode_island_index.htm

## South Carolina
**South Carolina Association of Nonprofit Organizations**
P.O. Box 11252
Columbia, SC 29211

Phone: (803) 929-0399
Fax: (803) 929-0173
E-mail: info@scanpo.org
Web: www.scanpo.org

## South Dakota

### South Dakota State Association
28670 181st Street
Pierre, SD 57501-5926
Phone: (605) 264-5350
Fax: N/A
E-mail: yack@sullybuttes.net, yack@sbtc.net
Web: N/A

### Nonprofit Management Institute
Dakota State University
Lowry Hall
820 N. Washington
Madison, SD 57042
Phone: (605) 256-5100
Fax: N/A
E-mail: jean.layton@dsu.edu
Web: www.departments.dsu.edu/npmi

## Tennessee

### Center for Nonprofit Management
44 Vantage Way, Suite 230
Nashville, TN 37228
Phone: (615) 259-0100
Fax: (615) 259-0400
E-mail: info@cnm.org
Web: www.cnm.org

## Texas

### Texas Association of Nonprofit Organizations
5930 Middle Fiskville Road, Box 51
Austin, TX 78752
Phone: (512) 223-7076
Fax: (512) 223-7210
E-mail: info@tano.org
Web: www.tano.org

**Texas Nonprofit Management Assistance Network**
9901 I-H 10 West, Suite 800
San Antonio, TX 78230
Phone: (866) 958-2845 (toll-free), (210) 558-2845
Fax: (210) 558-4207
E-mail: info@txnetwork.org
Web: www.txnetwork.org

## Utah

**Utah Nonprofits Association**
175 S. Main Street, Suite 750
Salt Lake City, UT 84111
Phone: (801) 596-1800
Fax: (801) 596-1806
E-mail: info@utahnonprofits.org
Web: www.utahnonprofits.org

## Vermont

**Vermont Alliance of Nonprofit Organizations**
299 North Winooski #3
Burlington, VT 05401
P.O. Box 8345
Burlington, VT 05402
Phone: (802) 862-0292
Fax: (802) 862-3549
E-mail: info@vanpo.org
Web: www.vanpo.org

## Virginia

**Virginia Network of Nonprofit Organizations**
2711 Buford Road
PMB # 339
Richmond, VA 23235-2433
Phone: (804) 794-8689
Fax: N/A
E-mail: info@vanno.org
Web: www.vanno.org

**Coalition of Virginia Nonprofits**
c/o Karin Talbert
Advantus Strategies

1011 East Main Street, Suite 400
Richmond, VA 23219
Phone: (804) 228-4509
Fax: N/A
E-mail: ktalbert@advantusstrategies.com
Web: www.cvnp.org

## Washington

**Northwest Nonprofit Resources**
P.O. Box 9066
Spokane, WA 99209-9066
Phone: (509) 325-4303
Fax: (509) 325-4260
E-mail: nnrinfo@nnr.org
Web: www.nnr.org

**Executive Alliance**
P.O. Box 22438
Seattle, WA 98122-0438
2014 East Madison, Suite 300
Seattle, WA 98122
Phone: (206) 328-3836
Fax: (206) 323-1017
E-mail: info@exec-alliance.org
Web: www.exec-alliance.org

## West Virginia

**Community Development Partnership of West Virginia**
P.O. Box 2204
Charleston, WV 25328-2204
1045 Bridge Road
Charleston, WV 25314
Phone: (304) 342-3754
Fax: (304) 342-1639
E-mail: info@cdpwv.org
Web: www.cdpwv.org

## Wisconsin

**The Nonprofit Center of Milwaukee**
2819 West Highland Boulevard
Milwaukee, WI 53208-3217

Phone: (414) 344-3933
Fax: (414) 344-7071
E-mail: info@nonprofitcentermilwaukee.org
Web: www.nonprofitcentermilwaukee.org

## Wyoming

**Wyoming Nonprofit Support Initiative**
c/o Lisa E. Johnson, Coordinator
Compass Communications
3896 Road 162
LaGrange, WY 82221
Phone: (307) 834-2293
Fax: (307) 834-2294
E-mail: lisa@compasswy.net
Web: www.compasswy.net/wano

HELP
HERE

# Appendix A

# Bylaws for a Nonprofit Corporation

## ARTICLE I. ORGANIZATION

1. The name of the organization shall be [NAME].
2. The organization shall have a seal which shall be in the following form [DESCRIBE].
3. The organization may at its pleasure by a vote of the membership body change its name.

## ARTICLE II. PURPOSES

The following are the purposes for which this organization has been organized: [DESCRIBE].

## ARTICLE III. MEMBERSHIP

Membership in this organization shall be open to all who [DESCRIBE].

## ARTICLE IV. MEETINGS

The annual membership meeting of this organization shall be held on the _____ day of [MONTH] each and every year, except if such day be a legal holiday, then and in that event, the Board of Directors shall fix the day but it shall not be more than two weeks from the date fixed by these Bylaws. The Secretary shall cause to be mailed to every member in good standing at his address as it appears in the membership roll book in this organization a notice telling the time and place of such annual meeting.

Regular meetings of this organization shall be held [LOCATION].

The presence of not less than _____ percent (____ %) of the members shall constitute a quorum and shall be necessary to conduct the business of this organization; but a lesser percentage may adjourn the meeting for a period of not more than _____ weeks from the date scheduled by these Bylaws and the secretary shall cause a notice of this scheduled meeting to be sent to all those members who were not present at the meeting originally called. A quorum as herein before set forth shall be required at any adjourned meeting.

Special meetings of this organization may be called by the president when he deems it for the best interest of the organization. Notices of such meeting shall be mailed to all members at their addresses as they appear in the membership roll book at least ten (10) days before the scheduled date set for such special meeting. Such notice shall state the reasons that such meeting has been called, the business to be transacted at such meeting and by whom it was called. At the request of _____ percent (_____ %) of the members of the Board of Directors or _____ percent (_____ %) of the members of the organization, the president shall cause a special meeting to be called but such request must be made in writing at least ten (10) days before the requested scheduled date.

No other business but that specified in the notice may be transacted at such special meeting without the unanimous consent of all present at such meeting.

## ARTICLE V. VOTING

At all meetings, except for the election of officers and directors, all votes shall be by voice. For election of officers, ballots shall be provided and there shall not appear any place on such ballot that might tend to indicate the person who cast such ballot.

At any regular or special meeting, if a majority so requires, any question may be voted upon in the manner and style provided for election of officers and directors.

At all votes by ballot the chairman of such meeting shall, prior to the commencement of balloting, appoint a committee of three who shall act as "Inspectors of Election" and who shall, at the conclusion of such balloting, certify in writing to the Chairman the results and the certified copy shall be physically affixed in the minute book to the minutes of that meeting.

No inspector of election shall be a candidate for office or shall be personally interested in the question voted upon.

## ARTICLE VI. ORDER OF BUSINESS

1. Roll Call.
2. Reading of the Minutes of the Preceding Meeting.
3. Reports of Committees.
4. Reports of Officers.
5. Old and Unfinished Business.
6. New Business.
7. Adjournment.

## ARTICLE VII. BOARD OF DIRECTORS

The business of this organization shall be managed by a Board of Directors consisting of [#] members, together with the officers of this organization. At least one of the directors elected shall be a resident of the State of _____ and a citizen of the United States.

The directors to be chosen for the ensuing year shall be chosen at the annual meeting of this organization in the same manner and style as the officers of this organization and they shall serve for a term of _____ years.

The Board of Directors shall have the control and management of the affairs and business of this organization. Such Board of Directors shall only act in the name of the organization when it shall be regularly convened by its chairman after due notice to all the directors of such meeting.

_____ percent (____ %) of the members of the Board of Directors shall constitute a quorum and the meetings of the Board of Directors shall be held regularly on the [DATE].

Each director shall have one vote and such voting may not be done by proxy.

The Board of Directors may make such rules and regulations covering its meetings as it may in its discretion determine necessary.

Vacancies in the Board of Directors shall be filled by a vote of the majority of the remaining members of the Board of Directors for the balance of the year.

The President of the organization by virtue of his office shall be Chairman of the Board of Directors.

The Board of Directors shall select from one of their members a secretary.

A director may be removed when sufficient cause exists for such removal.

The Board of Directors may entertain charges against any director. A director may be represented by counsel upon any removal hearing. The Board of Directors shall adopt such rules for this hearing as it may in its discretion consider necessary for the best interests of the organization.

## ARTICLE VIII. OFFICERS

The initial officers of the organization shall be as follows:

President:

Vice President:

Secretary:

Treasurer:

The President shall preside at all membership meetings.

He shall by virtue of his office be Chairman of the Board of Directors.

He shall present at each annual meeting of the organization an annual report of the work of the organization.

He shall appoint all committees, temporary or permanent.

He shall see that all books, reports, and certificates required by law are properly kept or filed.

He shall be one of the officers who may sign the checks or drafts of the organization.

He shall have such powers as may be reasonably construed as belonging to the chief executive of any organization.

The Vice President shall in the event of the absence or inability of the President to exercise his office become acting president of the organization with all the rights, privileges, and powers as if he had been the duly elected president.

The Secretary shall keep the minutes and records of the organization in appropriate books.

It shall be his duty to file any certificate required by any statute, federal or state.

He shall give and serve all notices to members of this organization.

He shall be the official custodian of the records and seal of this organization.

He may be one of the officers required to sign the checks and drafts of the organization.

He shall present to the membership at any meetings any communication addressed to him as Secretary of the organization.

He shall submit to the Board of Directors any communications that shall be addressed to him as Secretary of the organization.

He shall attend to all correspondence of the organization and shall exercise all duties incident to the office of Secretary.

The Treasurer shall have the care and custody of all monies belonging to the organization and shall be solely responsible for such monies or securities of the organization. He shall cause to be deposited in a regular business bank or trust company a sum not exceeding $ _____ and the balance of the funds of the organization shall be deposited in a savings bank except that the Board of Directors may cause such funds to be invested in such investments as shall be legal for a nonprofit corporation in this state.

He must be one of the officers who shall sign checks or drafts of the organization. No special fund may be set aside that shall make it unnecessary for the Treasurer to sign the checks issued upon it.

He shall render at stated periods as the Board of Directors shall determine a written account of the finances of the organization and such report shall be physically affixed to the minutes of the Board of Directors of such meeting.

He shall exercise all duties incident to the office of Treasurer.

Officers shall by virtue of their office be members of the Board of Directors. No officer shall for reason of his office be entitled to receive any salary or compensation, but nothing herein shall be construed to prevent an officer or director from receiving any compensation from the organization for duties other than as a director or officer.

## ARTICLE IX. SALARIES

The Board of Directors shall hire and fix the compensation of any and all employees which they in their discretion may determine to be necessary for the conduct of the business of the organization.

## ARTICLE X. COMMITTEES

All committees of this organization shall be appointed by the Board of Directors and their term of office shall be for a period of one year or less if sooner terminated by the action of the Board of Directors.

The permanent committees shall be: [DESCRIBE].

## ARTICLE XI. DUES

The dues of this organization shall be $ _____ per annum and shall be payable on [DATE].

## ARTICLE XII. AMENDMENTS

These bylaws may be altered, amended, repealed, or added to by an affirmative vote of not less than _____ percent (_____ %) of the members.

# Appendix B

# IRS Documents for Nonprofits

**Form 1023**
Application for Recognition of Exemption Under Section 501(c)(3) of the
Internal Revenue Code
This is a 26-page form, followed by a two-page checklist.
*www.irs.gov/pub/irs-pdf/f1023.pdf*

**Publication 557**
Tax-Exempt Status for Your Organization
This is a 63-page publication.
*www.irs.gov/pub/irs-pdf/p557.pdf*

# Appendix C

# Executive Director Evaluation Form

## Scoring Instructions

Please assess the Executive Director's job performance by scoring each item. The lowest score is 0 and connotes incompetence; a score of one (1) indicates fair performance with need for immediate improvement; two (2) good, with areas that need to be addressed; three (3) very good; four (4) superior; and five (5) indicates excellence. You may also circle DK (Don't Know) if you feel unprepared to evaluate an item. Please make comments in addition to the rating, especially if you circle 0, 1, or 2. The Executive Director wants and needs to know his/her level of performance.

The composite performance evaluation score shall be the average aggregate level of effectiveness compiled from the individual assessments of the Executive Committee.

| Area of Responsibility | Level of Effectiveness (Circle) |
|---|---|
| **A. Leadership** | |
| 1. Organizes effectively and plans ahead to meet the needs of the organization. | 0  1  2  3  4  5  6  DK |
| 2. Searches for and recognizes alternative solutions to problems. | 0  1  2  3  4  5  6  DK |
| 3. Deals with controversy effectively. | 0  1  2  3  4  5  6  DK |
| 4. Is aggressive about improving the organization. | 0  1  2  3  4  5  6  DK |
| 5. Exhibits high standards for the organization. | 0  1  2  3  4  5  6  DK |
| 6. Understands policy and exhibits consistency when interpreting and executing the intent of policies. | 0  1  2  3  4  5  6  DK |
| 7. Demonstrates ability to work well with individuals and with groups. | 0  1  2  3  4  5  6  DK |
| 8. Accepts responsibility for decisions and for subordinates' actions. | 0  1  2  3  4  5  6  DK |
| 9. Understands and keeps informed regarding all aspects of the internal management. | 0  1  2  3  4  5  6  DK |
| Comments: _____ _____ | |
| **B. Management** | |
| 1. Follows through on Executive Committee decisions and attends to details. | 0  1  2  3  4  5  6  DK |
| 2. Exercises fiscal responsibility through effective budget development, implementation, and control. | 0  1  2  3  4  5  6  DK |
| 3. Serves effectively as liaison with affiliates. | 0  1  2  3  4  5  6  DK |
| 4. Maintains positive working relationships with NREA Executive Committee Members. | 0  1  2  3  4  5  6  DK |
| 5. Maintains positive working relationships with Committee Chairs. | 0  1  2  3  4  5  6  DK |
| Comments: _____ _____ | |

| Area of Responsibility | Level of Effectiveness (Circle) |
|---|---|
| **C. Communications** | |
| 1. Writes and speaks effectively at all levels. | 0  1  2  3  4  5  6  DK |
| 2. Communicates the goals and objectives of the organization in meetings with the educational community at large. | 0  1  2  3  4  5  6  DK |
| 3. Responds to questions and requests in a timely manner. | 0  1  2  3  4  5  6  DK |
| 4. Shares information openly and frequently with Executive Committee, Affiliate CEOs, committee chairs, and members. | 0  1  2  3  4  5  6  DK |
| 5. Represents our organization through public appearances at national, state, and regional meetings. | 0  1  2  3  4  5  6  DK |
| 6. Involves the Executive Committee, committees, and other stakeholders in a "partnership" role in achieving the mission of the organization. | 0  1  2  3  4  5  6  DK |
| Comments: _____ _____ | |
| **D. Organizational Skills** | |
| 1. Designs and presents both short-range and long-range objectives based on our goals and objectives. Action plans are clear, articulate, and measurable and contain sufficient backup data to allow Executive Committee Members to properly make a decision. | 0  1  2  3  4  5  6  DK |
| 2. Plans, organizes, directs, controls, and evaluates action plans and programs as directed by policy and the Executive Committee. | 0  1  2  3  4  5  6  DK |
| 3. Uses his/her time effectively and efficiently when performing functions as Executive Director. | 0  1  2  3  4  5  6  DK |
| 4. Completes all tasks on time and in a professional manner. | 0  1  2  3  4  5  6  DK |
| 5. Is open to new ideas, accepts change, gives the ideas of others the benefit of the doubt, shares information with others, seeks guidance to improve, and remains flexible. | 0  1  2  3  4  5  6  DK |
| Comments: _____ _____ | |

| Area of Responsibility | Level of Effectiveness (Circle) |
|---|---|
| **E. Specific Program Area Evaluation of Performance** | |
| 1. Effectiveness in working with publications. | 0  1  2  3  4  5  6  DK |
| 2. Effectiveness in working with the annual convention. | 0  1  2  3  4  5  6  DK |
| 3. Add any other program area: _____ | 0  1  2  3  4  5  6  DK |
| Comments: _____ _____ | |
| **Overall Evaluation of Performance**  (not necessarily an average of above scores) | 0  1  2  3  4  5  6  DK |
| _____ Signature of Executive Committee Member completing evaluation. (Optional) | |
| Return Evaluation Form to the President, who will compile the evaluations into one report that will be shared with the full Executive Committee and presented to the Executive Director in a personal conference. Please return to reach the President by December 19, 2007. | |

# Index